FIELD&STREAM

WHITETAIL
HUNTING
GUIDE

FIELD & STREAM

WHITETAIL HUNTING GUIDE

SCOTT BESTUL & DAVE HURTEAU
AND THE EDITORS OF FIELD & STREAM

weldon**owen**

CONTENTS

001

KNOW THE 5 BASIC TYPES OF DEER HABITAT

If humans outlast deer, the paleozoologists of the future will sift through the fossil record and conclude that *Odocoileus* lived just about everywhere on this continent, from the wildest wilds to the back yard. Biologists have now identified more than 30 subspecies of whitetail alone that cover much of North and parts of South America. There's even a growing movement for those avid hunters who want to kill a "whitetail slam," consisting of the 8 major subspecies of America's deer. That's a fine idea, but no matter which species or subspecies you're pursuing, deer live in one of five major habitat types.

THE BIG WOODS The last stronghold of whitetails when European settlers nearly wiped them out, heavily forested regions of the North have continued to host solid populations of deer. But the big woods simply don't offer the abundance of food and edge habitat to support lots of deer. In addition, big-woods whitetails typically face a gauntlet of natural predators—such as coyote, wolf, bear, and bobcat—and tougher weather that limits their numbers. Big-woods bucks roam widely across large home ranges, so you usually need to cover some ground to tag one.

FARMLAND Whitetails were just about wiped out from America's breadbasket by the early 19th century, but when at last they bounced back, they did so like a roomful of rubber balls. So much so that when most folks envision deer hunting today, they see a hunter waiting by a woodlot adjacent to a field of corn, alfalfa, or soybeans. Lots of deer, plus lots of predictable food sources, plus broken wooded habitat all make it comparatively easy to pattern the daily movements of deer, which is the key to success on the farm.

PRAIRIE Technically, America has little true prairie habitat left, but we all know what we're talking about here: lots of real estate with durn few trees. In more recent decades, CRP acres, grassy swales, cattail sloughs, and cattle pasture have become prime real estate for the ever-adaptable whitetail. Riparian areas concentrate deer, but you're as likely to find a monster buck making a living in an abandoned ranch site. Out here in the great wide open, the hunter's challenge is plain to see: These deer can spot you from a long ways off.

MOUNTAINS When most hunters think "mountain" they're dreaming about sheep, goats, and elk. Drop down-slope just a bit, though, and you're in prime magazine-cover muley habitat. Descend farther down into the forested glades and foothills and— depending on where you live—you'll be bumping into blacktails and whitetails.

How many deer you encounter depends on what lies at the mountain's base. Sprawling ranches with crop fields means deer in abundance. Trees and more trees means big-woods conditions.

THE DESERT You might think rocks, sand, and prickly pears are too nasty for deer, but you would be wrong. In the sun-scorched regions of the Southwest lives one of the continent's most sought-after trophies, the Coues deer. This little whitetail ekes out a living in conditions that would cause a farmland buck dry up and blow away.

START WITH A SCOUTING WALK

There are more deer on the continent now than at any time in recent history, and yet we glimpse them only occasionally. Plain to see, however, is the evidence, or sign, they leave behind as they conduct their daily lives. To get close to their deer, most hunters rely on thorough scouting: the finding and interpreting of deer sign.

So, let's take a scouting walk.

You can start anywhere deer live, but the best place will be an obvious feeding area: a crop field, an oak ridge littered with acorns, or an old apple orchard. We'll start at an alfalfa field, along a perimeter, where the plants peter out into a strip of dirt and muddy tire tracks against the woods' edge. Here's what to look for.

1. RUBS

Follow the trail into the woods. Right there, just inside the edge, is a rub. Nothing screams "Buck!" like a hashed-up sapling. Folks once believed that bucks rubbed trees to rid their antlers of summer velvet; actually a buck makes most of his rubs after his antlers harden, as a kind of message to other bucks: "Here I am." Keep an eye out for other rubs, mostly on softwood saplings like pine, cedar, aspen, willow, and alder.

2. TRACKS AND TRAILS

The best place to find a deer track is in soft dirt, mud, or snow, and here is one at our field edge. It is basically heart-shaped, with a split down the middle, the narrow end pointing in the direction of travel. Follow it backward to where it joins others to form a narrow trail into the woods where multiple deer enter and/or exit the field. These trails wind through the woods and fields, connecting the places where deer sleep, drink, and eat. Whitetails create trails so they can dash through thick woods quickly to escape danger. Mule deer, typically found in more open terrain, use trails, too, but not as habitually.

3. BEDS

Where the trail eventually leads onto a grassy, brushy knoll is a kidney bean–shaped depression in the leaves where a deer rested. This is a bed. You'll find others in the places where deer feel the most secure, including ridge ends, thickets, blowdowns, and grassy lowlands. Large, lone beds in rugged terrain usually belong to bucks. Multiple beds of varying sizes tell you that a doe and fawn have been resting here together.

4. SCRAPES

Not far from the rub is an oval patch of exposed, moist dirt. This is a scrape. A whitetail buck made it by scraping away at the leaf litter using his front hooves, and then peeing in the dirt. Five or six feet above the scrape is a "licking" branch, which the buck has worked over with his mouth, eyes, and forehead, leaving a bunch of scent. The whole thing is another, more elaborate advertisement of his presence. Mule deer do not make scrapes.

5. DROPPINGS

A little farther along the trail, it looks like someone dumped a box of raisins; these are deer droppings. Keep an eye out for them whenever you scout. Lots of droppings mean you're standing in a spot where deer spend a lot of time, usually either a feeding or bedding area. Along with trails, the number of the droppings you see on a given property gives you a pretty good sense of the number of deer living there compared with other areas.

003 KNOW THE 5 BASIC METHODS

If you are new to deer hunting, pay close attention. This will be your foundation for understanding all of the advanced tactics described later. If you are a seasoned deer hunter, to borrow from Monty Python, skip a bit, brother.

STAND HUNTING

There are now so many deer roaming the country that if you stand still long enough, then sooner or later one is going to walk past you. That's an oversimplification, but nonetheless, it still goes a long way toward explaining why stand hunting has become the method of choice for most of today's deer hunters.

THE BASICS: You scout the woods to find a travel route used by deer and then set up downwind and wait for them to come to you. You can wait in a treestand 20 feet off the ground, in a pop-up blind on terra firma, or on a 5-gallon bucket tucked in some brush.

BEST USED: On the farm and the prairie, where small woodlots, draws, tree strips, hedgerows, fencelines, riverbottoms, and other broken cover tends to make deer movements more predictable.

STILL-HUNTING

This is a misnomer, sort of. The thing that makes still-hunting different from stand hunting is that you move. However, your periodic movements should be frequently interrupted by periods of standing—that's right—still.

THE BASICS: You go slinking through the woods, stopping often to listen and look, hoping to see deer before they detect you. Your pace depends on how promising the area looks. You might travel across an open hardwood flat devoid of deer sign in just a matter of minutes, hardly stopping. You might spend three hours tiptoeing through a brushy creekbottom, stopping for 15 to 30 minutes at a time.

BEST USED: Wherever there's enough cover to hide you. It's most common in the big woods, though, where deer are comparatively few and covering ground is going to up your odds of seeing one.

DRIVING

Pressured deer have this annoying habit of holing up in some impossible thicket from dawn to dusk, doing more or less nothing but watching out for you and staying out of your way. One solution is to barge right into that thicket and kick their butts up.

THE BASICS: A deer drive will involve anywhere from 2 to 10 or more hunters split into drivers and posters. First, the posters set up along natural escape routes downwind of any promising cover. The drivers then move into that cover from upwind, trying to push deer toward the posters for a shot. Deer drives need to be highly choreographed to ensure safety.

BEST USED: When deer are not moving on their own during daylight.

SPOT AND STALK

In some areas, deer, especially types like western whitetails, always seem to want to put themselves where they can see you coming from a half mile away at least. To have any chance, you need to see them first from farther than that.

THE BASICS: Use a spotting scope or binoculars to glass distant deer from a high vantage point or from your vehicle. Study the wind, terrain, and any cover to figure out how to sneak within gun or bow range without you being detected. Then carefully move in for the shot.

BEST USED: In open country: prairie hills, sage flats, grassland breaks, desert badlands, alpine slopes and meadows, and even farmland crop fields.

TRACKING

Bearded, wool-clad men follow hoof prints for miles into the snowy wilderness and then come back with a buck. Full of old-timey mystique, tracking is the most romantic of all the ways to kill a deer (though the deer may not feel that way).

THE BASICS: After a fresh snow, you drive along logging roads or go walking through the woods quickly to find a buck track. You follow it until the trail begins to meander or hook, meaning that the buck has stopped to feed or bed down. You slow to a crawl, and then comb the cover ahead and to the sides, hoping to spot the buck before he spots you.

BEST USED: In those large tracts of public forest or public-access timberlands where a hunter can follow a track all day long, and not encounter a single posted sign or even another hunter.

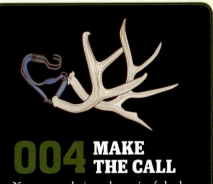

004 MAKE THE CALL

You can rattle (smash a pair of shed or synthetic antlers together to sound like two bucks fighting, which can attract other deer) and call (mimicking deer sounds, such as grunts and bleats) to great effect in conjunction with all the methods in item 003. Stand hunters will routinely rattle to draw a buck near and then grunt to stop him for a shot, for example. A tracker may track close to a bedded buck and then make a doe bleat to draw him out.

005 GEAR UP FOR DEER

You can go hunt deer with only a rifle, a cartridge, some clothes (please), and a pair of boots. But you will do better and have an easier time of it if you also have, at a minimum, these accessories.

BINOCULAR To see a deer before they see you. Get the best model that you can afford. A 10x42 binocular is best for open country. A light, compact 6x32 is perfect for tracking or still-hunting in the big woods. An 8x42 is a great all-purpose choice for deer hunting.

TREESTAND To get you above a deer's line of sight and to get your stink above its nose. It doesn't mean you won't get busted, but it can certainly help you. The more treestands you have, the better. If you own just one, get a climbing stand, which will help you out in hunting many different spots.

DEER CALLS To lure deer into shooting range or stop moving deer for a standing shot. At the very least, you should have a variable grunt call, a bleat call, and a set of rattling antlers.

THREE COMPASSES As Maine guide and friend Randy Flannery says, "A GPS is powered by batteries. But the Earth's magnetic field is powered by God." Why three? If one breaks, which do you trust?

ROPE If you are only going to carry one rope, make it 25 feet of ³/₈-inch braided poly rope. This is the most versatile for deer hunting—not too thick for pulling up a treestand, gun, or bow; not to thin for dragging out a buck.

KNIFE A full-tang drop-point with a fixed 2¹/₂- to 4-inch blade and wood or bone handle is the traditional choice. It's what I carry. That said, a folder with a good saw blade and extra tools sure is handy.

FOLDING SAW AND CLIPPERS To clear out shooting lanes, build a natural blind, quarter or bone out a buck in the backwoods, cut a limb for a drag handle, and the list goes on.

TWO HEADLAMPS Why headlamps? Because you are carrying too much other gear to have a hand left free to hold your flashlight. Why two? Because the first one is guaranteed to crap out at the very moment you need it most.

DAY OR FANNY PACK You need something to carry all this stuff in.

006 BE ULTRASAFE

In hunting, the soundest policy is to be overly cautious. The first rule in gun safety, for example, is to always treat a gun as if it were loaded even when you know perfectly well that it is not (see above). Why? Because it guards against stupidity. Why? Because the average person does something stupid between, like, 8 to 10 times a day. Just go on the Internet. As research for this, I killed a half hour on YouTube watching people fell trees directly onto their cars and houses.

The most dangerous thing in the deer woods is swagger, or overconfidence. Never assume that you can't do something dumb. Don't think, "I could never mistake a person for a deer" or "I could never pull the trigger without meaning to." Instead, double- and triple-check your target. Keep your safety on until the moment before you shoot. Always assume you could do something stupid, and guard against it by being overly cautious.

007 STRAP YOURSELF IN

One of the many sea changes in deer hunting during the last 20 years is a huge increase in the use of treestands. These treestands carry inherent risks, and you should know what they are. Should you fall out of a stand, there's a chance you will walk away a little bruised. There's a better chance you'll sprain or break something. And there's a real chance you will be eviscerated by your tree steps on the way down, break a leg when you hit the ground, and be left to die in the woods, alone.

So while we are on the subject of stupid things, I'll point out that one of the very dumbest a deer hunter can do is to go hunt from a treestand without using a safety harness, which, when attached to the tree, prevents you from falling. Last year, far fewer hunters were injured by bullets or broadheads than those who ended up injured in treestand accidents. Most of those injured were not wearing a harness.

008 COMMIT THESE 10 RULES TO MEMORY

Heard them before? Good. They should never escape your mind.

RULE 1 Assume every gun is loaded and treat it accordingly.

RULE 2 Unload your gun whenever it's not in use.

RULE 3 Be certain of your target and what lies beyond.

RULE 4 Keep your gun's safety on until you're ready to shoot.

RULE 5 Keep your finger off of the trigger until you're ready to shoot.

RULE 6 Wear at least the required amount of hunter-orange clothing.

RULE 7 Know your safe shooting lanes, especially when conducting a deer drive.

RULE 8 Never walk around with a nocked arrow.

RULE 9 Never drink and hunt.

RULE 10 Bring a cell phone and make sure someone knows where you are and when you'll be back.

009 NOW HEAR THIS

Remember those hearing tests you took as a kid? Someone would play a sound, and you'd put up your hand when you heard it. Well, researchers figured out how to do that with deer. They put deer of various ages into a soundproof booth and then hooked them to little electrodes measuring brain-wave activity. Computers then measured the frequency and volume of sound it took in order to register a bump in brain waves.

The conclusion? The average deer can hear high-frequency sounds better than we can (human hearing maxes out at 20,000 hertz; deer can hear up to 30,000 hertz), but the volume has to be turned up. Also, they are excellent at pinpointing the source of sound, thanks to their maneuverable ears. Other than that, deer actually don't hear much better than you or I do.

Like us, they hear moderate-frequency sounds best and virtually all the vocalizations they use to communicate with each other are in this range. And they get distracted by background noise in the woods, just like we do. So, you want to know how far off a deer can hear your calls, your rattling, or the sound of your foot cracking a stick? Have a buddy make those noises a set distance away. If you can hear it, so can a buck. If you can't, he probably can't either.

010 GET A GRIP ON DEER SENSES

After my rookie deer season, I was certain that bucks could see through hillsides, hear what I was thinking, and smell what I had for lunch from 100 yards away. We all tend to end up romanticizing the quarry. After all, giving the deer supernatural powers makes our successes more heroic and our failures more excusable. But let's get real here. If deer were that good, they'd all die of old age, and then we couldn't sell you this book. The truth is, deer senses are good, but not great. Only one—smell—is truly borderline otherworldly. The others . . . meh.

Maybe realizing your role in those hunting failures is no fun at all, but ignoring it can hamper your success. Yes, deer are sharp, and they're wary, and you should be careful. But you shouldn't let an exaggerated idea of their defenses keep you from making the aggressive moves sometimes needed to fill your tag.

011 KNOW THAT THE NOSE KNOWS

A deer's sense of smell is so spectacular that it's tough to quantify. But here's one good yardstick: Researchers estimate that we've got about 5 million olfactory receptors (neurons responsible for the detection of odor) in our noses. Bloodhounds—the legendary sniffers of dogdom—are thought to have 200 million. Meanwhile, deer have an estimated 297 million.

In other words, a deer's sense of smell is 60 times better than yours. In the proper conditions, a downwind deer can smell you from more than 300 yards away. And it can smell where you've been even long after you leave.

Not only can deer detect minute traces of odor, they can decipher many different scent types simultaneously. They can be snuffling acorns, whiffing nearby water, catching the scent of a coyote out in the woodlot across the field, and pinpointing the spot where you walked by an hour ago—all at the same time.

A multimillion-dollar industry exists with the sole purpose of defeating a deer's ability to smell a hunter—with little if any tangible success. In the end, a deer cannot see through hillsides or hear your thoughts. But it might be able to smell what you had for lunch. Above all, be careful of a deer's sensitive nose.

012 DON'T MOVE . . . OR WEAR BLUE

Deer have excellent peripheral vision and an outstanding ability to detect any motion. Their eyes have a high density of rods, a horizontal slit for a pupil, and a reflective layer on the retina (the tapetum lucidum), which allow them to see in the dark. They can also spot colors in the ultraviolet spectrum, which means that if your hunting garments contain any UV brighteners (as many do) or are blue, to deer you'll actually appear to glow in low light.

That's the good news for the deer. The bad: They can't see squat for detail. Researcher Gino D'Angelo actually devised an eye exam chart to measure the visual acuity of a captive doe named Nellie. D'Angelo found that Nellie's eyes were comparable to those of a human with 20/100 vision. Nellie, thank goodness, would flunk the vision portion of a driving test. Deer eyes are also fairly pathetic at depth perception. If you don camo and stand motionless against a broad tree, a deer staring in your direction from just 20 yards won't spot you.

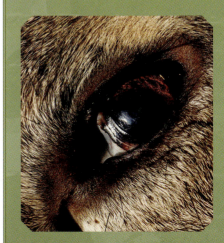

013 COVER YOUR SCENT

I was suspicious that cover scents really didn't do much for the hunter. With the help of a K-9 police dog, Ike, we ran a test to see how well hunters could hide using various scents. I was prepared for the exercise to be a yawner. What I got instead was a real eye-opener.

	COVER	RESULT
NO COVER	Our hunter dressed to hunt but with no scent-eliminating clothing and did not use any type of cover scent.	Ike found him in 6 seconds.
PINE & EARTH SCENT	We sprayed the hunter liberally with earth-scent spray.	Ike did not speed directly to the hunter's box. Rather, he ran past each enclosure once, then double-checked one before finding the hunter. Elapsed time: 25 seconds.
ACORN SCENT	We pinned acorn-scent wafers to the hunter's coat and misted him with acorn-based spray. I also soaked a rag with a synthetic acorn scent from an aerosol can.	Once again, Ike ran the entire course, scent-checking each box. Elapsed time before he found the hunter: 45 seconds.
SKUNK SCENT	The hunter used a small canister containing a cotton ball soaked with enough skunk scent to gag an outdoor writer.	It took Ike 45 seconds to find the hunter.

The goal is to delay the inevitable—to fool a buck's nose long enough to make a shot. Scent-reducing products failed utterly. Yet pine and earth scents, used as cover, were twice as effective as no cover scent, and acorn and skunk scents confused the dog for a half-minute longer.

014 CALL HIM OUT

The vast majority of deer hunters are very call-shy. In 40 years of hunting with and talking to fellow hunters, I'm continually surprised at how few of them try calling to whitetails even half as often as they really should (and almost no one tries talking to muleys). Meanwhile, deer of both species walk out of their lives that might otherwise have been lured into shooting range.

I know deer don't look or behave like raucous, vocal creatures. They don't howl like wolves, jabber like chimps, or gobble like turkeys. Aside from a very occasional warning snort, we just don't hear the deer "talk" to each other very much. The truth is that deer are actually pretty chatty.

Biologists have identified more than 90 different sounds made by whitetails alone. These vocalizations serve a wide variety of purposes: contact, reassurance, challenge, lust, alarm, and more. You don't need to mimic all of these sounds. Not by a long shot. Learning to do just the basics will definitely help you get closer to whitetails and muleys as you're on the hunt.

So here's what you do: Start by buying a variable grunt call that comes with an instructional DVD, and begin tinkering with the sounds at home. Then take your call to the woods and practice on deer you don't intend to shoot. Some of those deer will ignore you. Most will give you a look. Hardly any of them will spook. And some will come, looking for the doe, or fawn, or buck you're imitating. Then, the next time that you see a deer you do want to shoot that's walking out of your life, you'll know exactly what to do.

015 READ A TALE FROM THE TAIL

Whoever coined the old English proverb, "The eyes are the window to the soul" wasn't a deer hunter. With deer, it's all about the tail. You can often tell a whole lot about what a buck or doe is thinking or feeling just by watching its flag.

Relaxed and Droopy

"All's well in the world."

Almost Vertical and Flared

"I'm feeling a little edgy about something."

Vertical and Waving

"I'm outta here, and you other deer should run too."

Straight Out and Ruffled

"I'm dealing with some anger right now."

A Quick Twitch or Two

"I checked everything out; it's cool. No danger."

Continual Twitching

"Another week of deer flies, and I'm gonna need therapy."

Tucked Down Tight

"Pay no attention to me; I'm just looking for a rock to crawl under."

016 THINK DIFFERENT FOR BIG BUCKS

Older deer don't behave the same way as younger ones. Here's a breakdown of four key differences, and how to handle them.

MATURE BUCKS ARE LAZIER On south Texas' King Ranch, telemetry research showed that older bucks spent more time on their bellies than younger deer. "One old buck was only mobile about 19 percent of the time," says study leader Mickey Hellickson.
HUNT PLAN Set up closer to the buck's bedding area.

THEY'RE HOMEBODIES Hellickson's research also revealed that the longer a buck lives, the smaller his home range and core area become.
HUNT PLAN Find his pattern and be patient; he's around.

THEY'RE SEX MACHINES Most of us associate the rut with bucks chasing does across the landscape. Not so with older ones, says noted researcher Karl Miller. "Mature bucks have learned the signs indicating a doe is in heat. They wait for those signals before they make a move. They don't just run around hitting on everything in sight like teenagers."
HUNT PLAN Camp on the does during the rut, as well.

THEY MOVE LIKE GHOSTS An old buck knows to move around unnoticed. Instead of barging into a field to look for any does, he'll scent-check it from the downwind woods; instead of walking the spine of a ridge, he'll slink along the hidden sidehill.
HUNT PLAN Back off the main runways; Look for faint trails carving covert routes.

017 TAKE A PERSONALITY TEST

Deer are no different from dogs, cats, or horses—all animals to which we readily assign personality traits. Some bucks are brash and combative; others avoid conflict. Most are social, but there's always a shy loner who just doesn't play well with the others. Understanding these personality traits can make you a more successful deer hunter. If you know that a buck avoids confrontation, you'd never stake a buck decoy in front of him. Conversely, if you spot a belligerent brawler, you should feel confident challenging him with a loud grunt or snort-wheeze. Here's what you should look for.

SIGNS OF AN AGGRESSIVE BUCK

- Stares directly into the faces of other deer
- Lays his ears back and raises the hair on his front shoulders, back, and neck
- Moves toward other bucks that spar or fight
- Kicks or shoves other bucks, even while he's in velvet
- Runs bucks, does, and fawns off his feeding areas
- Has broken antler tines or visible scars
- Comes to the sound of rattling and calling

SIGNS OF A PASSIVE OR SUBMISSIVE BUCK

- Avoids eye contact with other bucks
- Moves to a different feeding area when another buck approaches
- Lowers his head and doesn't bristle his hair around other bucks
- Has a clean rack, with no broken tines
- Has a "pretty" face, with no scars or wounds
- Slinks away at the sound of rattling or buck vocalizations
- Tucks his tail

018 KNOW THE BIG 5 DEER FOODS

Just about every hunter knows that deer devour acorns, alfalfa, apples, corn, and soybeans. But to stay a step ahead of just about every hunter, you should also know the following about these five favorites.

 ACORNS Deer prefer acorns that fall without their caps, as these nuts tend to have fine, firm flesh. Those still sporting caps often have flesh that is punky or rotten.

 ALFALFA All deer love this tasty perennial member of the legume family, but never more so than when it's newly seeded. They'll hammer down a spring-planted field all fall and dig through deep snow to get to it in winter.

 APPLES Of course deer love the sugary fruit. But remember they'll keep hitting orchards to browse on the buds and twigs of these and other soft-mast trees long after the sweets are gone.

 CORN This is a game-changer. When the farmer fires up his combine, it's suddenly a race between deer and a whole host of other critters to clean up all that waste grain. That's why deer will temporarily abandon other foods to follow the combine. You should, too.

 SOYBEANS In early fall, deer crave this plant's green leaves, but once all that foliage turns yellow, the animals move on. They'll be back in winter to eat the beans.

019

SEEK SECONDARY FOODS

Given the choice between an acorn, an apple, and a red maple leaf, a deer will eat all three. You can try to explain to him that he has to choose one. But he won't listen, and it's not really in his nature anyway.

Deer are nibblers. Walking to and from primary feeding areas, they will nibble on a raspberry stem here, pluck an aspen leaf there, and maybe linger a while under a crab apple tree. Savvy hunters know this and keep track of these secondary food sources because their availability can dictate what path a deer chooses for its daily travels. Plus, when the savviest buck on your ground doesn't show in the crop field or food plot before dark, guess where he is: calmly mowing some secondary food source in the woods, waiting for dark before exposing himself. You might want to meet him there.

020 GO TO GRASS

High or low, and especially on flat ground, bedding bucks claim the thickest thickets: those impossible snags of briar and honeysuckle, the impenetrable low conifers, the jumble of blowdowns, vines, and saplings.

But there's another spot.

Hunters are quick to assume that deer bed in the woods. But when you don't find them there, go to grass. All kinds of grass. For a shy, old buck, there's nothing like a dry hummock swallowed up in cattails or loosestrife. Who's going to find him in a sea of switchgrass, or goldenrod, or CRP, or standing corn? Remember that some bucks use the woods for travel and tall grass for cover.

021

DON'T WALK PAST THAT PLOW

When those late-season bucks get pressured out of their usual haunts, they bed down where few hunters bother to look—right beneath our noses. Prime examples: shelterbelts near farmhouses; roadside ditches; abandoned homesteads; near farm equipment parked in the hedgerows and pastures; isolated patches of grass, cattails, or brush; backyard borders; right behind the barn; and right beside the hay bales.

022 LOOK HIGH AND LOW FOR BUCK BEDS

The fact that deer have been known to rest up on rooftops and down in some underground bunkers should tell you a couple of things about where they bed: (1) No spot is too odd to take a quick nap, and (2) you should start out by looking high and low.

In hill country, whitetail bucks love to bed up high where all the terrain is remote and rugged. Why go up there? Because most hunters don't like to have to climb hills, and because the location will offer the deer a good view of the few hunters who do.

Wilderness bucks will bed up high, too, but the old-time trackers swear that the biggest ones hunker down in low, heavy green growth: the cedar swamps, the spruce thickets, the close-growing pines. They may choose a somewhat elevated spot within the lowlands (a dry hummock in a swamp, a knoll within a spruce hollow) but it's relative.

Aside from muleys, you can find at least a few whitetails out on the open flats as well, where they hunker down in places like ditches, creekbeds, and swales—any depression that will help to keep their form below the sagebrush or broom grass and let them keep their eyes above or peering through the tops.

023 KNOW YOUR RUB

Once in a while, a whitetail buck makes a random rub, a light, incidental mark in a place where he's not likely to return. But far more often, rubs are purposeful and telling; they mean something—but what, exactly?

Bucks shred trees from the first hint of fall through the start of winter, in different places, and for different reasons.

Understanding what kind of rub you're looking at and how it should factor into your hunting plans can lead to more success in the field.

TYPE	DESCRIPTION	RUB I.D.	HUNTING SIGNIFICANCE
BOUNDARY RUB	Made by mature bucks in the early season as they begin to mark their breeding territory.	Look for large rubs along natural boundary lines, such as creeks, fencelines, and wooded edges.	These make good early-season treestand sites, often marking a route used about every three days in September.
TRAIL RUB	Made as a buck travels through his core area, typically from feed areas to bed.	Often found in a line, with clusters on either end nearest feed or bed.	Great pre-rut stand location. Determine the buck's direction by the side of the tree rubbed, and set up.
RUT RUB	Made during peak breeding by hormonally charged bucks near a hot doe.	Find shredded saplings or brush near doe bedding or feeding areas, with halfhearted scrapes nearby.	A fresh rut rub that's only days old? Set up now, or hang a stand and return in the morning.
COMMUNITY RUB	Worked by several bucks in high-traffic areas.	Found in staging areas or at the intersection of major trails; deeply gouged, typically on 3- to 5-inch-diameter trees.	Can be good spots to simply tag out, but not consistent for older bucks.
FIELD RUB	Marked at the edge of a field by early-season or pre-rut bucks approaching to feed.	Found by walking a field's edge, just inside the woods. They may or may not be part of a rub line.	This reveals at least one place where a buck enters a feeding area—but he may not step into the open until after dark.
GIANT RUB	Made only by the largest bucks to mark their core area, usually during the pre-rut.	Probably a trail rub—but a special one, blazed on 6- to 12-inch-diameter trees. They may be found in a line.	These are rare, revealing a 4- to 7-year-old buck's core area. Set up downwind and wait for a trophy buck.

As a buck ages, he becomes increasingly predictable about where he rubs, how he rubs, and what his rubs look like. And you can use that information to set up an ambush. Here are five things to look for when unraveling the rub-making habits of an older buck.

TREE SPECIES Most whitetails pick on trees that have sappy, aromatic bark, including sassafras, aspen, cedar, and pine. Once a buck gets older, however, he'll often pick one particular species to the exclusion of all others. I've hunted bucks with a preference for ash, white cedar, or even wooden fence posts.

TREE SIZE Bucks usually favor tree trunks of a specific size. One of my old buddies tells the story of hunting a huge buck that tortured any red pine with a 3-inch diameter—because they were the biggest trees he could fit between his near-touching antler tips.

TERRAIN AND COVER Bucks can be very particular about where they choose to rub. For example, I've hunted bucks that have made rubs only in the swamps, even though their favorite tree species also grows on uplands.

UNIQUE ARTISTRY Funky racks will make for one-of-a-kind rubs. One buck I tracked all season had a forked brow tine on his right-side antlers that left an unmistakable gouge. Really wide bucks often wreak collateral damage on nearby saplings and brush. Some unique antler artistry is obvious; some not so much. So make sure to get in the habit of inspecting rubs closely.

RUB HEIGHT Some bucks only rub down low, topping out at just 2 feet above the ground. Others crane their necks skyward and end up leaving elk-high markings at 5 or 6 feet up. Find a bunch of the latter and you can bet that they were made by the same buck—and that he'd look good on your wall.

MAKER'S MARKS

STUDY EACH RUB FOR HINTS ABOUT A BUCK'S TREE-RAKING HABITS, FOR EXAMPLE:

1. He likes cedars; look for more of that species.
2. He prefers to rub a fairly thick trunk.
3. His wide rack scars adjacent saplings.
4. He rubs fairly high—likely a good-size buck.

025 SCORE DURING SCRAPE WEEK

Hunting over scrapes can be maddening throughout much of the season. Research has shown that whitetails visit them mostly at night. Also, it's not at all uncommon for bucks to make one casually and then never revisit. And once the peak rut begins, even the hottest scrapes can suddenly go stone cold. For a short time each fall, however, scrape hunting can be fantastic. The key is to get out into the woods before the peak breeding period.

The absolute prime opportunity to hunt over this sign will last about a week, and straddles the seeking and chasing phases of the rut, starting about a week and a half before breeding crests. If you locate fresh scrapes then, the odds are very good that a buck will be hitting them while the sun is up. Even better, you're almost sure to find them: Bucks open up more scrapes during this roughly weeklong period than at any other time during the year. Also, with their testosterone levels rising, these boys spend more time on their hooves during daylight, opening up and checking out scrapes, and cruising for does—but they remain within their home ranges and along their familiar routes. Such predictability increases your chances for a successful ambush.

Don't expect these scrapes to stay hot, though. One of the biggest reasons hunters get skunked over this sign is that they will hunt it too late, when bucks have switched their focus from pawing at dirt to running down does.

Finally, it's important to understand that even during this seven-day window, some scrapes are better than others. Bucks are more likely to revisit those situated in or near secure cover. Overgrown logging roads that are surrounded by woods are great spots, as are wooded ridgetops, river bottoms, and evergreen stands. Whenever you find one scrape, take the time to look for another, and another, along a line that reveals a deer's travel route.

026 GET THE DIRT ON SCRAPES

Check out those scrapes carefully, since all manner of different factors will then dictate different hunting strategies.

	DESCRIPTIONS	HUNT PLAN
OPEN SCRAPES	Look for these scrapes in or along the edges of fields, clear-cuts, and other openings. They begin popping up during the pre-rut and are typically worked at night.	Back off and seek corresponding buck sign in a nearby staging area with good cover. This is where you can ambush a mature buck before nightfall.
HIDDEN SCRAPES	As the pre-rut progresses, deer start hitting more and more of these scrapes within the woods. The thicker the cover, the more likely bucks are to work them during shooting light.	Setting up between the scrape and a known bedding area can be a deadly tactic now. Hang a scent wick soaked with regular buck urine and call with passive contact grunts.
CHASE SCRAPES	Certain scrapes get really hot during the seeking and chasing phases. Fresh dirt will be tossed everywhere, the licking branch will be mangled, and nearby saplings will be newly savaged.	Locating your stand right over the scrape can pay off big as big bucks begin cruising for receptive does. Get aggressive. Put out estrous doe scent and hit the rattling horns.
RUT SCRAPES	Most scrapes are more or less abandoned once breeding begins in earnest. One key exception, however, is buck sign near doe bedding areas.	Hang your stand overlooking scrapes on the downwind edge of a doe bedding area. A combination of doe bleats and estrous scent can bring bucks trotting into shooting range now.
LATE SCRAPES	When unbred does come into heat, roughly 28 days after the primary rut, bucks may reopen scrapes. These scrapes are comparatively scant but well worth locating.	Set up within shooting distance and use tending grunts, doe bleats, and snort-wheezes to attract or challenge bucks competing for the few estrous does left.

027

FIND EARLY RUBS AND SCRAPES

Are you waiting for late October to scout for buck sign, when it's most abundant and easiest to find? Well, stop that. You need to look for it earlier. Why? Because according to the latest research, the first rubs and scrapes, which often show up before October, are usually made by the biggest bucks.

On average, a male whitetail makes between 300 and 400 rubs per fall, but younger bucks open only about half as many as older bucks do. What's more, whereas young bucks don't go making hard-antler rubs until late October, the mature whitetails begin savaging tree saplings and de-barking thigh-thick trunks almost immediately after antler shed in late August or early September.

Scraping, too, can begin right after velvet shed, and the older bucks create roughly 85 percent of all scrapes. In other words, find those early rubs and scrapes, and you've probably found a good-size buck.

028 USE THE OLD .30-06 TRICK

A classic trick of the old-time trackers is to lay a .30-06 round across the width of a deer track. If the hoofprint is as wide or wider than the cartridge, it belongs to a good-size buck. Fortunately, a .25-06 Rem., .257 Weatherby Mag., .264 Win. Mag, .270 Win., .280 Rem., 7mm Rem. Mag, .300 Win. Mag, .35 Whelen, and other cartridges of similar length will do the trick, too.

029 TAKE A SURVEY

It's not as easy a thing as counting, say, sheep, but by using a method developed in the late 1960s by the Wisconsin Department of Natural Resources, you can, roughly, count out the deer in your hunting area. Here's how.

STEP 1 Head to your hunting area, pick a starting point, and then walk 450 yards in a straight line as you count out the deer trails you pass (include logging roads and people paths if they show deer tracks).

STEP 2 Stop, move over 200 yards, and head back in the direction you came on a line parallel to the first pass, counting all the way.

STEP 3 Move over another 200 yards and then make another pass. Continue doing so until you've completed at least four passes.

STEP 4 When you're done, divide the number of deer trails that you counted by the number of passes you made. For example, if you have counted 30 trails and you made 10 passes, then the number you need to remember is 3.

If the number you come up with is 2, 3, or 4, you have roughly 5 to 7 deer per square mile in the hunting area. If the number is 5, 6, or 7, you can estimate 15 to 20 deer for every square mile. If your number is 8 or more, count your blessings.

F&S POLL — WHERE TO AIM

Bowhunters all agree: Aim behind the shoulder. Gun hunters, on the other hand, hotly debate the best shot placement on a broadside deer. One camp shoots through the shoulders to drop a buck fast. Most shoot behind the shoulder, which ruins less meat. And some still favor the neck shot. So we showed our online readers this illustration and asked: With a gun, where would you shoot?

Here's how more than 2,000 readers voted:

Other: 3%

Neck: 4%

Behind the shoulder crease: 65%

Shoulder: 28%

030 FIND A MONSTER BUCK AT HOME

You might just have a monster buck living right under your nose. If you haven't seen him, it's probably just because he doesn't get around a whole lot.

For years, researchers and hunters have assumed that as a buck matures, his home range gets bigger. But recently, Mickey Hellickson, the former chief biologist on south Texas's well-known King Ranch, took a new look at some old data, and he found that just the opposite was true: The longer a buck lives, the more his territory actually shrinks.

In 1992, Hellickson's team fitted 125 whitetail bucks with telemetry collars and monitored their locations weekly for three years. Technically, the study was ended in 1995, but it's still yielding up eye-popping information today. After analyzing all his original data specifically for buck range by age class, he published the study results in the June–July 2010 installment of *Quality Whitetails* magazine, revealing that "old" bucks (7 ½ or older) have the smallest home ranges, averaging 1,055 acres—less than half that of "young" bucks (2 ½ and younger) and at least 25 percent smaller than that of "middle-aged" (3- and 4-year-olds) and "mature bucks" (5 and 6).

But here's the real kicker: Territory shrinkage holds for core areas, too, with old bucks averaging just 151 acres. And prior to the pre-rut, while deer are still in their summer pattern, home ranges and core areas tend to be significantly smaller than the average. The oldest buck there on your property might also be the biggest homebody. And during the early season, his primary haunt may be no bigger than one corner of your hunting ground.

031 CRASH THE BACHELOR PARTY

Several bucks out feeding together in a summer alfalfa field isn't coincidence; it's a bachelor group. And if you're smart, when you spot these boys hanging out on your hunting ground, you'll bring out your set of binoculars, set up a safe distance away, and spy on the party. Here are the things you should look for.

POSTURING One reason you see bucks band together now is to start working out dominance. These guys will compete for breeding rights in the fall, and answering some basic "Who's the boss?" questions now decreases the chance of a serious fight later between familiar bucks. The process starts low-key while the bucks are still in velvet. Posturing, shoving, hoof-flailing—all of this is more attitude than action, but it does give some insight into individual buck personalities.

FIGHTS Bachelor bucks do party on after velvet shed, but as their testosterone levels continue rising, the competition will grow more fierce—typical guys. Suddenly one buck cops an attitude and another ups the challenge. And with no more tender tines to protect, they'll be using their antlers as the weapons they are. If the boys just walk up to each other and lower heads, then the sparring will rarely get serious. But if they

sidestep, circle, bristling the hair on their backs and rolling their eyes back, sparring can get ugly. Many hunters believe bucks save serious fights for the rut; in fact some of the fiercest battles take place now. Pay attention, and you'll assemble critical data about how certain bucks will respond later when you call or rattle to them.

THE BREAKUP Even the best of parties have to end. As late summer gives way to early fall, the appearance of that bachelor group at evening food sources—once as predictable as a noon whistle—becomes haphazard. Suddenly there are three bucks instead of five. Or a single buck feeds in

one corner of the field while two former buddies stay in another. In any case, the once-cohesive unit goes the same way as all boy bands—each member splitting off of the group to go solo.

The good news is that most will stay in the general neighborhood. You can keep on watching this field, but also check other top food sources. Set up trail cameras and make midday scouting runs with an eye for new rubs and scrapes. If the habitat is good, odds are you'll find the old boys.

032 WAIT FOR THE PRODIGAL BUCK

If you've nailed down that big buck's core area, the rut can leave you feeling like the prodigal son's father. Sunday-school lessons a little hazy? Just like the rutting buck, the prodigal son left home, vamoosed, went out to sow his wild oats. But he returned, and so will your buck, most likely.

What's the proof? In a recent study at Chesapeake Farms, by wildlife manager Mark Conner, bucks began moving more extensively as the rut kicked in, frequently abandoning their original core areas and occasionally roaming beyond their home ranges. But here's the kicker: Most of them returned within 8 to 32 hours. "If a buck was faithful to a core area in the pre-rut," said Conner, "he was coming back." Also, since the activity recorded by sensors on the GPS collars indicated that returning bucks were mostly idle, it's safe to assume that those bucks came back to their core areas to rest up. And there's one more big thing. Are you sitting down? The data also showed that most bucks made the return trip during daylight hours.

In other words, two of the most widely held assumptions—first, that rutting bucks will not return to their core areas until the rut is over, and second, that hunting core areas is a waste of time during the rut—are dead wrong. So if you're among the many hard-core whitetail hunters who work hard at nailing down the core areas of individual bucks, you can rejoice! The rut isn't a time of despair. You just need to keep the faith, brother. Set up in a funnel leading in and out of a core area's best bedding cover, be prepared to sit all day, and wait your buck out. According to this study, there's a great chance you'll kill something far bigger than the fatted calf.

033 PICK YOUR FIGHTS

If you think the peak of the rut is the best time to rattle in a buck, you're right—but maybe not the biggest buck. This is just one of the things that whitetail researcher Mickey Hellickson proved during a two-year study conducted on an 8,000-acre Texas ranch. Hellickson placed observers in elevated blinds, and then had someone rattle a set of antlers at ground level. His teams conducted three 10-minute rattling sessions in a wide variety of areas and in all kinds of weather. Here are five key lessons they learned that you can put to use for yourself this fall.

1. GET UP EARLY Rattling sessions in the morning got the most responses from bucks, followed by afternoons. Midday was the worst time to rattle.

2. CHECK THE WEATHER Low wind speed, cool temps, and 75 percent cloud cover proved to be the ideal conditions for productive rattling.

3. WAIT FOR A GIANT During the pre-rut, the first responders were the yearling bucks, followed by some of the old bucks. During the peak rut, middle-aged bucks (3 ½ to 4 ½ years of age) responded best. The really old boys came in during the post-rut period.

4. PLAY IT LOUD, MOSTLY As a rule, loud rattling brought in the most bucks, as you might expect—with one fascinating exception. When truly old bucks came to the antlers in the post-rut, softer rattling (ticking the horns and grinding the bases) was more effective.

5. GET HIGH Ground-level rattlers only laid eyes on 33 percent of the bucks that were spotted by the elevated observers, which just goes to show that many bucks may approach the sounds of a fight but not totally commit. This makes rattling from a treestand a good idea.

034 KNOW YOUR DEER

A little less than 50 subspecies of whitetail, blacktail, and mule deer range from just below the Arctic Circle to the southern tip of South America, weighing from a mere 80 pounds to more than 400, and eating everything from lichen to cactus. Here is a breakdown of the whitetail types in the United States and Canada.

WHITETAIL DEER

- 1. Virginia whitetail – *Odocoileus virginianus virginianus*
- 2. Northern whitetail (the largest subspecies) – *O. v. borealis*
- 3. Carmen Mountains Jorge deer – *O. v. carminis*
- 4. Key deer – *O. v. clavium*
- 5. Coues deer – *O. v. couesi*
- 6. Dakota whitetail – *O. v. dacotensis*
- 7. Hilton Head Island whitetail – *O. v. hiltonensis*
- 8. Columbian whitetail – *O. v. leucurus*
- 9. Kansas whitetail – *O. v. macrourus*
- 10. Avery Island whitetail – *O. v. mcilhennyi*
- 11. Northwest whitetail – *O. v. ochrourus*
- 12. Florida coastal whitetail – *O. v. osceola*
- 13. Florida whitetail – *O. v. seminolus*
- 14. Texas whitetail – *O. v. texanus*

035 DON'T GIVE UP

A classic excuses for not seeing a buck is, "He's gone nocturnal." A smart buck may reduce daytime activity as a response to hunting pressure; very few, if any, become completely nocturnal. During the rut, even the mature bucks pursue estrous does, no matter the sun's position. And in very cold winter weather, midday feeding might become a biological imperative.

036 CHECK THE DEER FORECAST

SUNNY AND HOT Expect deer to bed out of the sun—on north-facing slopes or in deep shade where the prevailing wind helps keep bugs at bay. Swamps and creek bottoms can also offer cooler air and access to drinking water. Any activity will take place at the edges of daylight.

LIGHT RAIN AND FALLING TEMPERATURES Deer won't mind just a little rain or drizzle, and when these cold-front conditions snap a prolonged hot-and-dry spell, they can spur deer movement.

COLD, CALM, CLEAR These are ideal conditions for good daytime deer activity. After a front ushers in cooler temperatures, atmospheric conditions stabilize, and the barometer starts rising again, it's time to climb into your treestand.

HEAVY PRECIPITATION This will put deer down for a while. Expect them to hole up in protective cover and stay there for as long as the rain, snow, or sleet lasts. They'll be hungry when conditions normalize.

SUNNY AND COLD Look for deer to bed on south-facing slopes, where they are able to soak in what little warmth the winter sun offers. Bitterly cold temps will force them to hit top food sources hard for the energy needed to stay warm.

BREEZY AND COLD A top priority for winter deer is to stay out of the cold wind, which quickly robs them of the little heat their bodies can produce. When a bitter breeze stirs, late-season deer will stick to hollows, bowls, lee-side slopes, and low, protective cover areas.

037 STUDY THE STORM

When chimney smoke bends to the ground and swirling winds send leaves spiraling, take notice; a storm is brewing. Deer seem to know when bad weather is coming, and act differently before, during, and after a storm. You should prepare to react, too.

BEFORE THE STORM Deer don't eat in a downpour or a driving snow, so they fill up before bad weather arrives. If a storm starts in the afternoon, expect deer to feed late into the morning. If it's coming at night, expect them to eat in early afternoon. If it's very powerful—especially a snowstorm—moving in, gear up for an all-day vigil near a prime feeding area.

DURING THE STORM In pouring rain, icy sleet, or a harsh blizzard, deer head to sheltered areas and stay put. In hilly terrain, deer hole up in gullies, hollows, and lee-side slopes with good overhead cover, such as conifer stands. In flat areas or farmland, they go to low, thick cover, such as a dry knoll in a cedar swamp or a cattail slough where the bitter wind blows over the tops.

AFTER THE STORM What deer do after bad weather depends on the type of storm. Heavy rains rarely keep deer down for long and may bring better hunting with cooler temps. The same applies for a snowstorm that dumps 3 to 10 inches of fresh flakes and ushers in cold, calm conditions. This can make a half-beaten late-season hunter feel brand new. But lingering cold winds can keep deer in their sheltered areas, browsing nearby until conditions stabilize. Even in this situation, however, there is an upside: In the meantime, the deer get very hungry. Once conditions calm down, deer will eagerly hit choice feeding areas.

038 NAIL DOWN NORTHERN DEER YARDS

In these days of whitetail abundance, it's difficult to imagine the survival of the species hinging on one tree. But in the early 20th century, when the only solid populations of whitetails lived in the vast forests of the northern United States, deer numbers could have crashed further were it not for swamps dominated by northern white cedar.

The browse and thermal protection offered by cedar swamps were so critical to their winter survival that whitetails would migrate great distances—sometimes 30 miles or more—to reach them in the early days of winter. Cedar swamps could hold hundreds of deer at high densities per square mile.

Cedar and hemlock swamps offering thermal protection and winter food continue to be critical habitat for whitetails in northern forest that migrate to traditional yarding areas for the worst of winter. Hunting for deer in yards, when deep snow makes them vulnerable, is often frowned upon, but interception of deer moving through traditional migration routes generally isn't.

039 BONE UP ON WINTER BEDDING AREAS

Many whitetails, particularly those in farmland environments, don't have to make a dramatic adjustment to make their winter lives easier. Just bedding down and loafing in an area that offers a thermal advantage can make all the difference. One of the textbook places for this is a south-facing slope, which offers more sun as well as protection from prevailing—and often bitter—northwest winds. Often these slopes host cedar or pines that offer security cover and additional protection from the wind, but sunbathing winter deer will readily bed in brush or grasses if necessary. Whitetails may hit the same food sources that they visited a month before, but the advantages gained by this southern-slope bedding shift are also undeniable.

040 STUDY THE WINTER SHIFT

For northern deer, winter is often a brutal season. As deer food sources diminish, intense cold forces these animals to live off of fat reserves to maintain body heat. Meanwhile, deep snow not only means difficult travel, it makes deer vulnerable to predators as well. To endure this harsh season, most deer will make some sort of shift in territory. From the subtle to the dramatic, these winter movements give deer an edge in the survival game. Understanding how deer in your area make their winter shift helps you to anticipate their late-season movements. When the hunting is over, the very same knowledge will make you a better shed finder and habitat manager, too.

041 FIND THOSE WINTER BEDS

If you're aspiring to be among the growing number of fanatical deer hunters, then you must realize that the end of deer season is not an end at all but the beginning of the next hunting season. In other words, get ready for about seven or eight months of scouting around.

The day after the last day is the first day (you with me?) when it won't really matter whether or not you spook any deer. This is critically important since it means that you are suddenly free to go parading into those recently unapproachable bedding areas in order to figure out exactly where all those elusive deer are sleeping.

So as soon as the season ends, go for a hike. Scour every potential bedding area, looking for both buck and doe beds.

When you're done you'll know precisely where all of those deer were bedding down on your property during the late season. If the food sources stay mostly the same, it's a pretty good bet those deer will lie down in the very same spots once again during the last few weeks of next year's season. And you'll have them pegged.

042 GET ON THE WHITE TRACK

When there's snow on the ground, every step that a deer takes is a matter of public record, and nothing gives you a better big-picture view of how deer are using your property than following their hoofprints during the off-season. This is equally true whether you're scouting in the dead of winter or in early spring.

Changing food sources can affect the deer's movements to a degree, but terrain and cover will mostly dictate the ways in which deer navigate the landscape, and these factors stay largely the same all year. Thus, the snow-covered off-season is the perfect time to identify any funnels, pinch points, and other travel patterns.

While following in their footsteps, pay careful attention to the line of their tracks ahead. When you see the trail swinging around the head of a wash, sidehilling a particular ridge, or slipping over a certain saddle, that's something to make a note of. Deer may not always be moving through that area, but when they are out, they'll use the same corridors—and you'll know right where to hang your stand.

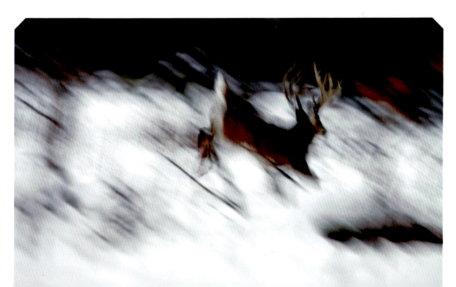

043 SPRING INTO ACTION

If you have just a single chance to go scouting before next deer season, do it in March. There is no other time when so many clues about local deer behavior are laid so bare before you, and spooking bucks is a nonissue this far in advance of fall. For many of us, March is a time when snow is here and gone—and then sometimes here once again—but within this muddled transition from winter to spring lie the secrets to what those deer are doing right now and what they were up to last fall.

WHEN THERE'S SNOW, LOOK FOR

TRACKS In March, as in winter, off-season tracks (1) show you generally how deer are moving through your hunting area.

BEDS Spring bedding areas (2) may not be used in fall; on the other hand, they may. So be sure to add them to your inventory.

RUBS Rub lines (3) reveal specific travel routes taken by bucks during the hunting season. As long as the snow isn't too deep, last fall's hashed trees should be plain to see. Follow every rub line that you can decipher, making note of any ambush points. Watch for clusters of rubs, too, that indicate an area that gets a lot of use.

WHEN THE SNOW MELTS, LOOK FOR

SCRAPES Last fall's scrapes (4) are plain for you to see now too, and it's important that you categorize them quickly. Small scrapes and any made near food sources were done at night or on a whim. Instead, focus on large scrapes or concentrations of scrapes located in the timber, under a licking branch or branches. Select and mark a good stand tree and keep it in mind for next fall.

SECONDARY TRAILS More mature bucks don't leave rubs and scrapes everywhere they go, and they will commonly travel off the beaten path (5). Keep an eye out for fainter trails that intersect main trails near a food source or ones that veer just off the obvious runways. I walk every minor trail I can find, and inevitably I end up discovering a covert route that I have been missing for years, even on familiar ground.

FALL BEDS Yes, beds, again (6), but this is a little complicated. See the next item for details.

044 GET THE RIGHT STAND FOR YOU

No specific number of stands is just right—or ever enough. That said, these five types are great to have. Don't go skimping on the climbing stands; you really get what you pay for here. You can, however, find mid-priced ladder stands and even dirt-cheap hang-ons that work great. Just shop carefully

LADDER It's a pain to put up, but nothing will be easier or safer to hunt from. Perfect for a reliable hotspot that you can drive right up to.

STEALTH CLIMBER For exploring new, remote spots, nothing gets you in more quietly and up more quickly than an ultralight compact climber.

COMFY CLIMBER Suppose that you find a public-land hotspot that's begging for an all-day sit. This is when a little more padding will be worth the extra weight.

STEALTH HANG-ON You need a featherweight model that goes up fast for short-term sets where you can't use a climber.

COMFY HANG-ON Use this type for long sits in consistent hotspots where it's not practical to carry in a ladder.

046

HANG A TREESTAND IN 7 MINUTES

How long does it take for you to hang a lock-on stand? Twenty minutes? A half hour? More? Well, you can do it much faster. All you need is the right equipment and a method that keeps you from going up and down the tree 15 times. Last year, I posted a short video series on our site's Whitetail 365 blog (which you can see by Googling the headline above), in which I safely hang a stand and am ready to hunt in about 7 minutes.

It's not a race, of course (no matter how much it may appear to be so in the video), but it is handy to be able to shave minutes from your setup time.

Bring a lightweight lock-on stand with a cinch strap (as opposed to a ratchet type strap). It's just easier to pull up and set. You're also going to need to get three or four climbing sticks. They're faster and safer than using tree steps.

Make sure everything you may need—extra sticks, clippers, a saw, safety line—is readily at hand in a fanny pack or pockets. Now you're ready to start climbing.

Tie one end of a pull-up rope to your stand and the other to your safety harness. Do the same with your gun or bow if you plan to hunt now.

Attach one climbing stick to the base of the tree while your feet are on the ground. Grab the second's strap in one hand. Clip the third to your safety harness.

Climb halfway up the first stick. Attach the second stick. Take the third one from your harness and attach it. Add a couple of tree steps if needed. Pull up the stand and hang it. Get in. Pull up your gun or bow. Sit down. Hunt.

045

PICK THE PERFECT STAND TREE

Whenever possible, you should pick a tree that is perpendicularly downwind and well off of the animals' direction of travel to avoid their line of sight and to keep passing deer from winding you. For bowhunting, it should be located 12 to 20 yards from the best sign. Farther makes for a long shot; shorter makes for a steep angle. For gun hunting, the tree should be as far from the hottest sign as you can get and still have a high-odds shot, ideally one with a long view of the terrain. Make sure it offers an entry and egress that won't spook the deer. Your choice needs to be wide enough to hide your silhouette but narrow enough that you can wrap your arms around it for easier climbing and stand hanging. And finally, ensure that it has several trunks, branches, or forks to give cover and for hanging equipment.

047 FIND FALL BEDS IN SPRING

When spring's upstart sun melts the last of the snow and you finally have to face the fact that hunting season is still six months away, don't wallow in despair. Instead, remind yourself that this is the perfect time to nail down last fall's buck bedding areas. This simple research mission will greatly increase your odds of tagging a brute when the hunt resumes.

Before we go any further, let's get something straight: Unlike at other times of the year, the bedding area that you are seeking is not going to be something that's the size of a yoga mat. If you do find any of those individual beds preserved from last fall, that's great.

For the most part, however, bucks don't bed down in the exact same spot day after day. Given this fact, your goal is to locate a larger area—maybe a quarter acre up to a few acres in size—where a buck repeatedly rests in a few, maybe up to a dozen, spots.

The easiest way to find this magic spot is to follow a rub line away from a known fall feeding area. You'll typically see lots of sign in or just off the grub and fewer traces as you progress. When rubs start growing more abundant again, you're close. Once you find clusters of savaged saplings, then you're there.

Comb the area around this spot for any supporting signs, but especially beds. You won't always find them. (In pine duff the depressions are barely noticeable.) After rising from bed, the first thing a buck does is relieve himself; second, he rubs a tree. That means droppings and rubs are key. If you're lacking for good rub lines to follow, simply walk straight toward the most likely bedding cover.

For each buck bedding area that you discover, mark a good stand tree along a rub line or funnel leading to the lair. Then go ahead and trim shooting lanes, leave, and stay out. This last step is essential. For trophy bucks to establish predictable bed-to-feed patterns that you can capitalize on later, their sanctuaries need to go largely undisturbed for some time.

048 HANG IT AND HUNT IT

About ten years ago, Scott Bestul introduced me to the nutty, nutty method called hang-and-hunt, which seems to be the popular thing with all the bowhunting kids these days. When he told me that he routinely goes into an area, hangs a lock-on stand, hunts in that spot, and then breaks it all down immediately afterward, I said, "You're a freaking nut."

For hit-and-run deer hunts, I have always been more of a climbing-stand guy—plus, it used to take me a half hour (on a good day) to hang a lock-on. But if you can learn, as I have, to hang a stand in just a few minutes, the upside of using a lock-on for one-stop hunts becomes clear: Not limited (as you are with a climber) to straight, branchless trees, you can hunt from whatever perch puts you in the absolute best spot to fill your tag.

049 FOLLOW THE GROUND RULES

Brooks Johnson, the cofounder of Primos Double Bull Blinds, has been hunting from pop-up blinds exclusively since 1995. Here are the tricks he has discovered for fooling whitetails on their level.

USE THE 50-YARD RULE If a deer won't have a visual line to your blind until he's 50 yards away from it, you need to completely camouflage the hide into the natural cover. At that distance, a buck won't tolerate being surprised by any hint of a foreign object.

USE THE 100-YARD RULE On the other hand, if a buck has a visual line to the blind from 100 yards or more—such as in a field setup—set the blind in the wide open so he can see it from every side. Put the blind out a day or two ahead of time so the deer have a chance to get used to it.

HIDE THE ROOF The roofline's hard edge is one of the first things that a buck spots. Cut some limbs and put them on top of it.

CLOSE THE WINDOWS You want it to be as dark as possible inside. If there's too much light, deer will see you when you move, even a little.

WEAR BLACK The goal of camo is to match the background. When you're in a ground blind, your surroundings are dark.

HIT THE NET Use shoot-through netting on the windows. It camouflages the dark holes of blind openings as well as concealing your movement.

STAKE A FAKE Whenever possible, use a buck decoy to attract nearby deer and thus pull their attention away from your blind.

050 CUT IT OUT!

Want to start up a hot deer-camp debate? Ask all your buddies how aggressively they trim the shooting lanes. Half will insist that sparing the saw spoils the shot. The rest will argue that too much hacking spooks deer and ruins the spot.

Who's correct? Both are—but only about half the time. A simple either-or approach won't allow for the fact that proper trimming is highly situational; it should really depend on the specifics of each hunting setup.

About half of the stands I hang are located near a terrain funnel or pinch point that isn't apt to change, like the head of a wash, a bench or saddle in hill country, or a brushy fenceline or a creek bottom that's connecting crop fields. These spots will dictate deer movements year after year, so I thoroughly brush them. After getting the landowner's permission, I use a small chain saw to remove the scrub trees and major limbs that might block a shot. The obvious alterations or residual scent might temporarily spook deer, but I do know they'll be back; I'll have plenty of chances to hunt them.

Ideally, I do such brushing in the off-season. But even after the opener, I've found I can hunt these sets within just a couple of days, as they are usually situated a modest distance from any buck bedding or core areas. If I'm worried about my leaving too much scent, I'll trim just prior to a rain.

051 GET GOOD GLASS CHEAP

This is the Golden Age of Cheap Glass, in which the quality of low- to mid-priced ($200 to $400) scopes and binoculars has shot right through the rafters. The trend really became unmistakable for me in 2009 when I picked up the then-new Bushnell Legend Ultra HD 10x42 binocular and said, "Holy s**t! These can't possibly cost $240!" But they do.

Today, Bushnell, Nikon, Leupold, Vortex, and others make shockingly good glass in this price range. It might not paint the world in a magical light that gives even your thoughts more clarity, like the really high-end models (Swarovski, Zeiss, Leica) can, and which is great to have if you can afford it. But, if not, these will perform admirably.

052 ASSEMBLE A $1,000 DEER COMBO

What's remarkable is that today's deer hunter can get a very capable combo—rifle, scope, and binocular—for under $1,000. Even the long-range deer hunter, who typically has to spend more to spot and drop faraway critters in the great wide open of the West, can come in close to a cool grand.

On a recent eastern Oregon mule deer hunt, for example, I carried a Weatherby Vanguard Series 2 Synthetic in .257 Weatherby Magnum (about $490 street price and guaranteed to shoot inside a minute of angle) topped with a 4.5-14x44 mm Bushnell Legend Ultra HD Scope (about $280 street price) and a Bushnell Legend Ultra HD 10x42 binocular (about $240 street price). That comes to $1,010. I've used guns and glass costing much more, and I don't believe any of them would have served me much better as a practical matter.

053 ACHIEVE AFFORDABLE ACCURACY

By happy coincidence, this is also the Hyper-Accuracy for Peanuts era of bolt-action rifles. I declare this because, after spotting an emerging trend at the 2012 Shot Show, David E. Petzal and I tested five new or newish bolt-action rifles that retail for around $500 or less. At the range, two of the five guns averaged three-shot groups of nearly a minute of angle. The other three shot well under—under, I say—a minute of angle. And they just so happened to be the three least expensive guns.

They were, in ascending order by accuracy:

THOMPSON CENTER VENTURE

AVERAGE GROUP: .816"
SMALLEST GROUP: .446"

GOOD

RUGER AMERICAN RIFLE

AVERAGE GROUP: .780"
SMALLEST GROUP: .372"

BETTER

MARLIN X7

AVERAGE GROUP: .713"
SMALLEST GROUP: .200"

BEST

Each of these rifles has a real-world price tag of under $400, and the most accurate, the Marlin, sells at most shops for a paltry $330 or so. Not too long ago, sub-minute-of-angle performance cost big bucks, and so the dawning of the HAFP era may bring pain to those who've already spent thousands for gilt-edged accuracy. However, especially in the wake of the Great Recession, it should bring unbridled jubilation to any practical-minded hunter looking to buy a tack-driving deer rifle today.

054 HUNT DEER WITH AN AR

The first hunting AR-15s to hit the market were works in progress at best. But with the feedback from a growing number of AR-toting deer hunters, the manufacturers are starting to get it all right. The latest stocks are adjustable; triggers are infinitely crisper; and hand guards are free of Picatinny rails except where needed. What's more, as the best new hunting ARs have slimmed down to a nimble 7 pounds or less, the number of available calibers has been beefed up to include a handful of deer-perfect rounds, including the 6.5 Grendel, 6.8 mm SPC, .30 RAR, and .300 Blackout. None of these three excellent examples is cheap, but you only need to buy a new upper to make it your plinker or varmint rifle, too.

AMBUSH FIREARMS 6.8 This camo carbine weighs just 6 pounds and is chambered for 6.8 mm SPC, which has become a huge hit with hunters wanting a low-recoil, moderate-range whitetail cartridge. The Magpul MOE stock is adjustable, and the Geissele SSA trigger is just this side of perfect. The hammer-forged barrel is guaranteed to produce MOA accuracy.

ALEXANDER ARMS LIGHTWEIGHT 18-INCH 6.5 GRENDEL Pushing 120- to 130-grain bullets, the 6.5 mm Grendel has mild recoil but enough horsepower for any whitetail, even at long ranges. This 7.5-pound rifle has a lightweight, carbon-fiber fore-end and adjustable stock, a great trigger, and a quality barrel cut to just the right length to make it a great all-around deer rifle.

PRIMARY WEAPON SYSTEMS MK116 MOD 1 RIFLE .300 BLK Weighing just 6 pounds, 7 ounces, the MK116 Mod 1 is lightweight, quick-handling, and is available in one of the newest AR cartridges, the .300 Blackout, which shines as a mid-range, light-recoil round for whitetails and uses standard .223/5.56 mm magazines to boot. The Geissele trigger is outstanding; the Magpul MOE stock and grip make for comfortable shooting; and the free-floating fore-end enhances accuracy.

BEST DEER CARTRIDGES

F&S POLL

If we are not debating the best deer rifles on the Whitetail 365 blog, we are debating the best deer cartridges. In 2010 we launched our first March bracket with the Sweet Sixteen of Deer Cartridges, as in general-purpose rifle cartridges. We put 16 popular rounds head-to-head, and readers voted for the winners. Here's how the Final Four went down.

.270 WSM	.30-06
.30-06	
CHAMPION .30-06	
.270 WIN	
.270 WIN	.308

055 CHOOSE THE RIGHT BULLET

In a perfect world, every deer bullet would expand quickly, penetrate just enough to pass through, and then, having expended all its energy in the deer, fall straight to the ground next to a big, bright blood trail. Alas, perfect bullet performance is tricky, because it relies on a host of variables, including bullet construction, velocity, shot placement, and more. The best you can do is get the right bullet for the type of deer hunting you'll be doing. Here's a basic rundown.

JACKETED LEAD-CORE	A basic, inexpensive deer bullet, made with a soft lead core and a thin brass or copper jacket that gets thicker toward the bottom. It's designed for rapid expansion and moderate penetration.	**BEST FOR** Slow- to moderate-velocity rounds at moderate ranges–a good basic bullet for most deer hunting.	**DRAWBACK** At very high velocities, it's apt to fly apart and penetrate little.
BONDED LEAD-CORE	Same as above, except that the lead core is chemically bonded to the jacket, resulting in better weight retention and thus more penetration.	**BEST FOR** Higher-velocity rounds at moderate to long ranges.	**DRAWBACK** They cost a bit more.
CONVENTIONAL CONTROLLED-EXPANSION	Has reliable moderate expansion with a wide range of velocities, and retains 70 to 90 percent of original weight for deep penetration. Often high ballistic coefficients and can be exceedingly accurate.	**BEST FOR** High-velocity rounds in open country, where you don't know if your buck will show at 40 yards or 400 yards.	**DRAWBACK** They cost a lot more and simply aren't necessary for many deer-hunting scenarios.
ALL-COPPER CONTROLLED-EXPANSION	Also built for reliable moderate expansion, these bullets provide maximum penetration through the toughest hide and bone. These, too, tend to be highly efficient and accurate.	**BEST FOR** Same as above, or if you have to shoot through a Volkswagen to hit your deer. Or if you end up hunting lead-free.	**DRAWBACK** Generally the most expensive bullet you can buy–and often not necessary for deer.

056 CHOOSE THE RIGHT COMPOUND BOW

A compound bow is a simple pulley-and-lever system. The energy that you get out is proportional to what you put into it. (Today's bows are better in part because they're more efficient.) A faster bow is generally harder to draw. And some of the things that make it fast also make it harder to shoot well. Getting the right bow means understanding the tradeoffs.

ACCURACY Archers always argue over the lethality of various broadheads as well as the relative speed, smoothness, and quietness of different bows. None of it matters if you can't hit what you're aiming at, but with perfect accuracy you could kill deer with a sharpened oil dipstick shot from a washtub bass. As a rule, less-skilled archers need more forgiving bows, usually longer and heavier (more stable and easier to hold on target) or slower (easier to hold at full draw without creeping forward, and apt to have a longer brace height). Good shooters need less forgiveness, and usually shoot something shorter, lighter, and faster. The trick is finding a bow you can potentially shoot accurately and then shoot until you do.

SPEED If you can shoot it accurately—a big *if*—a faster bow has major advantages. It can shoot a flatter arrow, making the exact range estimation less critical. If it fires the average hunting arrow of around 400 grains at an honest 280 fps or faster, then it should let you shoot out to 30 yards with one pin without having to hold outside the vitals, simplifying things enormously in the field. The best advantage to a blazing bow is that you can shoot a heavier arrow with a heavier head without losing too much trajectory, for more momentum and better penetration. Neither makes any difference if you make a perfect shot, but if you screw up, they can turn an otherwise nonlethal shot into a filled tag.

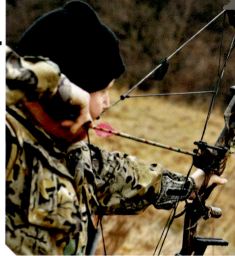

057

DON'T TRADE ACCURACY FOR SPEED

You can set up a bow to maximize one or the other—speed or accuracy. Unless you are such a good shot that you can give up a little accuracy and still be hell on wheels out in the deer woods, favor accuracy. Here are a pair of examples of how this works in real life.

CRANK IT DOWN Cranking up your bow's draw weight increases the arrow speed. But if you shoot better with it turned down—then turn it down.

DRAW SHORT Some hunters shoot a draw length that is too long but don't want to give up any of their speed by shortening it. Just give it up. Too long a draw puts too much of your face against the bowstring, can make it difficult to maintain a consistent anchor point, and can cause you to lock your bow arm out straight, as well as creep forward with your string arm. It's not worth it. Not sure if your draw is too long? See a good bow-shop pro.

058 SHOOT A STICK AND STRING

Every now and then, I hear a hunter claim that traditional archery—hunting using a longbow or recurve—is "coming back." In truth, stick-bow shooting never went away. Custom bowyers are so swamped by orders that it can take more than a year to get your hands on one of their bows. Graceful and full of character, longbows and recurves are fun to shoot and certainly deadly on deer.

But behind the romance, there's a hard truth: It's not easy to shoot a stick bow well. The key is to learn the proper form, and then practice—a lot. So let's get started.

STANCE Forget the straight-up compound posture. Assuming you shoot right-handed, point your left foot at a slight angle toward the target and bend slightly at the knees.

GRIP This is the only similarity to shooting a compound. Keep the grip on your lower palm, against bone, and relax your fingers.

ANCHOR You'll need to find a consistent anchor point, but it's rarely the same one you'd use to shoot a compound. I like my middle finger to hit the corner of my mouth at full draw. I also put the tip of my nose on the string.

DRAW Turn the top limb slightly to the right (again, for righties), which will keep the arrow on the rest and give you a better sight picture. Pull back smoothly using your back and shoulder muscles as your eyes focus on the target.

RELEASE When you reach your anchor, your eyes should be burning a hole into the target. Keep that focus while you relax your fingers and let the arrow go. Follow through by holding your form and looking the arrow into the target.

059 GET OFF THE BENCH

This is the drill that will make you into a true marksman. Go to the range and burn some ammo, shooting at National Rifle Association 50-yard slow-fire bull's-eye targets, which have an 8-inch bull's-eye. Assuming you've sighted in your rifle, get off the bench. Why? Because shooting from a perfect rest will not be the same as shooting under most field conditions.

Working at 50 yards, firing offhand, take 10 shots, never giving yourself more than three seconds to get the rifle up, aim, and shoot. Next, fire five shots kneeling, taking no more than five seconds per shot. Finally, if you'll hunt from a treestand, take another five while sitting in a chair. For these, you take your time. This is precision shooting.

Take all 20 of these shots twice a week. When you can get all of your shots from kneeling and sitting, and get nine out of 10 from offhand, in the black, then it's time to move back to 100 yards and repeat.

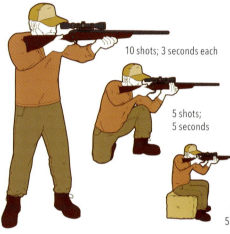

10 shots; 3 seconds each

5 shots; 5 seconds

5 shots; take your time

50 YARDS

060 KNOW YOUR LIMITS

Unless you're truly exceptional, you'll learn in a hurry that you can't do the same things with a stick bow that you can with a compound. Your effective range will likely be 25 yards or less. Your arrows will travel at half the speed of a garden-variety compound. You won't draw as heavy a bow. Some hunters, acknowledging these truths, save their traditional bow for the range—or for the curio wall of their man cave, which is perfectly fine. Others embrace the challenge and limitations of traditional archery and recognize these bows for the incredible hunting tools they are. I shot one of my largest whitetails at 15 yards with a recurve a year ago; it's probably the buck I'm most proud of in 40 years of whitetail hunting.

061 KEEP SHOOTING SIMPLE

Perhaps you've noticed the newest legion of long-range riflemen on TV spinning their turret-mounted knobs before taking a shot, or you've gazed into the latest range-compensating scope and figured, *that must be the big secret.*

But hold on just a minute. I know some spectacular riflemen who will turn target turrets just as fast as I can recall a drop chart. But they are very, very few. And I have tried out range-compensating scope reticles that do function wonderfully . . . as long as you remember to crank them up to full power. Theoretically, either can save you the inherent imprecision of holding off your target.

On the other hand: [1] In the real world, big bucks are not in the habit of milling around stupidly while you spin knobs and count the hashes. [2] Without a heap of practice, trying to do either can go very wrong while your brain is swimming in adrenalin. [3] Most of you needn't ever worry about holding off.

A great many deer hunters simply don't have the time to shoot a bunch. If that's you, it's probably best if you keep your shots at deer within 300 yards—and almost any reasonably flat-shooting round sighted a little high at 100 will keep you well in the hair at that range. As for that small remainder who can reasonably shoot to 400, there is no shortage of very flat-shooting rounds—even some non-magnum rounds—that can do the same. This takes care of about 99 percent of you, and the 1 percent who can and do hit reliably beyond 400 don't need my advice.

Take your typical 115-grain .25-06 bullet. Sighted 3 inches high at 100, it is damn near dead on at 300 and drops only about 10 inches at 400. A 130-grain .270 WSM sighted 2.5 inches high will drop about the same. Meanwhile, the chest area of a good whitetail buck, measured from back to brisket, will span about 20 inches. In other words, no need to aim out of the hair.

The best system is the simplest: Shoot your rifle with your chosen hunting round to learn the point of impact at various ranges. (Don't rely on ballistics charts.) Then write it down and either memorize it or tape it to the rifle's butt stock. In the field, range your target, or estimate the range if you must, and then simply remember or glance down to see that you need to hold 4 inches high at 350, or 10 at 400, or whatever. Compensate and shoot. That's it.

062 DON'T GET TOO FAR AWAY

Extreme long-range shooting, which we define here as "anywhere between 300 yards and halfway to the dwarf planet Ceres," seems to be all the rage these days, particularly for hunters seeking mule deer and western whitetails. A very small handful of folks can do this kind of shooting ethically. For anyone else who might be thinking, *That doesn't look so hard,* it's important to at least try to cure yourself of that notion. Indeed, every deer hunter should learn to access his or her real-world accuracy at a variety of ranges.

So first, let's agree that before pulling the trigger on any poor deer that stands to give it all up for you, there should be a high probability of making a shot that will end things quickly. Agreed? Okay, now do this:

STEP 1 Starting at 150 yards, shoot five shots from a kneeling position (with or without sticks, as is your normal practice in the field) at a target with an 8-inch bull. If you put four out of five in the black, move back 25 yards and do it again. Once you do reach the point when you can't put four out of five in the black, that's it; you're done. Your previous distance is the maximum at which you should shoot kneeling at a deer.

STEP 2 Now do it sitting (with or without sticks), starting out at 200 yards and moving back 25 yards at a time.

STEP 3 Finally, go prone (with or without bipod or pack, as is your normal practice), starting at 250 yards and moving back 50 yards at a time. There, that should cure you.

063 GET GOOD FORM

Learning and keeping good form is what will get you to shoot your bow better. Practice the following routine until you can do it in your sleep.

Stand with your feet shoulder-width apart and perpendicular to the target. Lots of guys like to turn their lead toe open a bit for better stability and balance.

Keep a consistent anchor point. Find where your release hand will comfortably meet your face at full draw; put it in the same spot every time. And because two anchor points are better than one, drop your nose down on the string or use a kisser button.

Don't hold the grip like a hammer; this introduces torque. Instead, turn your palm up and rest the grip against the bony heel of your palm, between the fleshy pads. Keep your fingers safely under the shelf and well away from the arrow, but leave your hand relaxed and open as you shoot.

At full draw, continuously push toward the target with your bow arm and pull away with your string arm as you squeeze the trigger. Follow through smoothly. Try not to move your head, drop your bow arm, or grab too quickly for the bow's handle.

064 PAY ATTENTION TO THE DETAILS

Here are some little things that can make a big difference in how well you shoot. Keep an eye on them and watch your accuracy improve.

SHORTEN YOUR RELEASE If you're tripping your release trigger with the tip of an extended index finger, stop. This tends to make you slap at the thing. Shorten your release aid, instead, so that at full draw you are able to curl your index finger around the trigger at about the middle joint. This will make it easier to squeeze the trigger smoothly and with better control.

FLOAT THE PIN AND SQUEEZE You wouldn't think that letting your sight pin float on, off, and around the bull while you squeeze the trigger could possibly tighten your groups. But it does, like magic. Stop trying to hold the pin perfectly still on your mark, which is often not possible anyway. Instead, let it float and then squeeze—slow and steady does it.

WATCH THE ARROW Eyeing the shaft all the way to the target through the sight-pin bracket during your practice sessions promotes better follow-through and keeps you from dropping your bow arm during the shot.

CHECK YOUR BUBBLE LEVEL The bubble level on your sight reveals the cant and torque you're putting on your bow—both of which are accuracy killers. Always use it on the practice range because it helps form good habits. Glance at the bubble as part of your pre-shot routine, then adjust the bow as necessary, and your groups will shrink like magic.

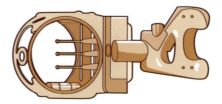

065 GO LONG

Hitting a target at 100 yards with a bow is not so difficult as you think. Try it out. Not only does long-range practice make shots at hunting ranges seem like gimmes but it also magnifies subtle mistakes in shooting form. If you mess up your form at 30 yards, you may still be in the kill zone. If you mess up at 100 yards, you'll miss the whole damn target and lose a $12 arrow. This forces you to bear down and shoot well.

WEEK 1 At these ranges, concentrate on perfecting the fundamentals of good form.

WEEK 2 You may have to fine-tune your sight as you move back.

WEEK 3 You don't have to shoot at 100 yards. If you can't hit the target consistently beyond 70 yards, for example, stop at 70. It will still be great practice.

LAST DAY Hit a deer target from here, and your confidence will soar at field ranges.

WEEK 4 Way out here, it's especially critical to push and pull through the shot and to make a smooth release.

LONG-SHOT REGIMEN
HERE'S HOW TO HIT AT 100 BEFORE THE OPENER:

WEEK 1
Review the basic shooting tips on the facing page, while shooting three arrows at 20 yards. Step out to 30 and do it again. Now go to 40, take a deep breath, remember the basics, and shoot five arrows. Relax and shoot five more. Do this whole routine two or three times a day.

WEEK 2
Do the same as above, but this time make the distances 30, 40, and 50 yards.

WEEK 3
With your stance, anchor point, and grip perfected, shoot at 50, 60, and 70 yards, focusing on two things: (A) pushing and pulling through the shot; and (B) floating the pin as you squeeze the trigger.

WEEK 4
Same routine, but at 70, 80, and 90 yards. On the last day, replace the block target with a good-size buck target, step back to 100, and double-lung the thing.

066

MATCH THE ARROW SPINE

Two bows with the same draw length and weight may require different arrow spines for optimum accuracy. Any reputable bow shop will have access to a spine calculator. But if you're buying online, make sure you speak with a tech to match the spine with your bow's specs for best performance.

067 MAKE THE MOST OF PRACTICE

As with most things in life, the main thing to getting better at shooting with a bow is practice, practice, and (yep, you guessed it) more practice. Here are a few things that will boost your effectiveness.

PRACTICE IN LOW LIGHT Most bow shots you'll have at mature whitetail bucks happen during either the first or the final ticks of daylight, when sight pins dim and your peep sight seems to shrink. So devote some practice time to those opening and closing minutes of legal light in your area to prepare for this crunch time and to learn your maximum effective range in low light. And count on it being much tighter than you probably expect.

MAKE THE FIRST SHOT COUNT Repetitive practice is fine for perfecting form. But few bucks will give you a second shot, let alone a fifth. About a month prior to the opener, start off each morning by shooting just a single, broadhead-tipped hunting arrow. Pick a distance, visualize a hunting scenario, and shoot. Then walk away. Increase the difficulty as the season nears, and you'll be ready for that make-or-break shot.

SHOOT FOR SOMETHING A friendly gamble helps teach you to steel your nerves while at full draw. Bet a quarter per arrow with your buddies during your backyard practice and let the smack talk flow freely.

SHOOT THE HEART AND LUNGS

- ⌖ SHOT WITH A BOW OR A GUN
- ⌖ SHOT WITH A GUN

068 SHOOT FOR THE HEART AND LUNGS

The heart-lung area—located between and extending behind the front shoulders of a broadside deer—is the deadliest target for the vast majority of shooters. That's because if you make the shot, the deer is dead, period, and because it is the most easily made of the deadly shots.

Compared to the throat patch, lower neck, or head (God forbid), the heart-lung area is a larger target—about the size of a rugby ball with its nose wedged tightly between the deer's shoulder blades. Pop it, and you go home with venison.

With a gun and a good bullet you can shoot through the shoulder or brisket to get to those vitals, making broadside, quartering-away, quartering-to, or head-on shots all quite lethal. An arrow, however, may or may not penetrate through the shoulder, and to kill quickly it must either pierce the heart or puncture both lungs. This means that the broadside and quartering-away shots are the only real high-odds opportunities. So, be sure to wait for them.

069

TAKE THE NECK SHOT, IF YOU MUST

In his book *Shots at Whitetails*, Larry Koller praised the throat patch shot to gun hunters. "Any shot into the upper third of the deer's neck," he wrote, "is so decisive in result that this writer has yet to hear of a deer moving from its tracks after being hit in this area . . . [L]ower neck shots seem to have much the same effect on deer as the quick removal of a head with an axe has on the Thanksgiving turkey." A good neck shot does the job, but it's a small target for most hunters If all you have is a neck shot, and you're confident you can make it, fine. Otherwise, shoot for the heart-lung area.

070 WATCH THAT FRONT SHOULDER, BOWHUNTERS

I hear a lot of deer hunting stories from fellow bowhunters. Inevitably, a small but not insignificant percentage of them start something like this: "I thought I hit him perfectly, right behind the shoulder . . ." Yet the hunter couldn't have hit the deer perfectly because he either failed to recover the animal or only found it after an arduous tracking job.

Bowhunters need to redefine a "perfect" shot, which has likely been influenced by the 3-D targets we use for practice. Most full-body deer targets sport a neat little 10-ring immediately behind the "animal's" front elbow, over an area that would result in a heart-shot deer. No doubt, putting an arrow in a real buck here is a quick kill.

But there is something critically wrong with this shot: It leaves too little room for error. And when your eyes are tearing from the cold and your knees wobbling under the influence of buck fever, errors are all too common in the field. If you do not make this "perfect" shot perfectly, the likelihood of disaster becomes roughly a coin toss. If you miss too far back, you'll probably be okay. But if you miss forward, the arrow will find the shoulder, the brisket, or leg— none of which are at all good.

The solution is simple. Forget the 10-ring on a 3-D target. Erase that "perfect" shot from your mind and replace it with one a few inches farther back—that is, roughly on the center of the lungs, which are about the size of a basketball, perhaps, or slightly smaller.

If your arrow flies perfectly, your deer is dead. If the shot is a little off, there's a lot of lung surrounding your new 10-ring. Get anywhere close to it with a sharp broadhead and you will find your deer.

071 AGE A BUCK IN THE FIELD

Most beginners look at a buck's antlers and put him in one of three categories: small, big, and holy crap! But if you're concerned about your deer herd's age-structure, you need to study up on a deer's body size and proportion, too, as these are even better indicators of age. Here's what to look for.

1 ½ YEARS OLD Sometimes called a "yearling," this buck is wearing his first set of antlers, which can range from a pair of tiny spikes to a small 8- or 10-point rack. Either way, the rack will be fairly thin, with a spread less than 14 inches. The body is the surest clue: This buck will be slim and long-legged, much like a doe. His neck won't swell during the rut.

2 ½ YEARS OLD In some areas, a 2 ½-year- old buck can carry a Pope and Young record-book rack. But the body will tell you he's still got some growing to do. His belly is sleek with no sag, and he'll still look "leggy" compared to an older buck. Some neck swelling will occur during the rut, but his slim face should tip you off to his youth.

3 ½ YEARS OLD The antlers of many 3 ½-year-old bucks will make P&Y records and then some. Though he's well muscled (a common analogy is to that of a thoroughbred racehorse) and he has a beefy neck, he doesn't have the bulk of a truly old deer. The biggest tip-off here: a distinct junction where the neck meets the shoulders, which seems to get lost in older deer.

4 ½ YEARS OLD This buck is fully mature, with a rack that is wide, high, and massive. During the rut, his neck will swell to meet the shoulders seamlessly, giving him a bull-like appearance. His rounded belly and his chest make his legs appear short. In all but the most tightly managed properties, this buck here is the epitome of what a whitetail can be. So quit looking and take your shot!

072 FORM A HUNTING GROUP

Unless you're fairly well heeled, paying for even a modest lease will require one or more partners. Take your time choosing them. Every lease member will be equal parts hunting buddy, coworker, and business partner, and one individual lacking in any category can make for a long and frustrating experience. Here are some guidelines.

SELECT CORE PARTNERS Three to six members is a good, manageable number to begin with. It's easier to add people if you need or want to expand your group than it is to get rid of a bad egg.

DECIDE ON FINANCES Members should agree on a per-hunter cap on costs. This will help as you shop for ground and decide how to budget for projects such as food-plot seed and equipment like stands, tools, signs, etc.

ESTABLISH GOALS Are you leasing land simply to secure access and get to enjoy an undisturbed hunt, or do you want to manage for trophies? Agreeing on your goals ahead of time will establish harmony among group members and can help define the size and location of the property you seek.

SET BYLAWS They aid communication and make things fair to every member. For instance, you'll need to establish workdays for scouting, hanging stands, planting food plots, etc. And you'll need to come up with a guest policy. Will any friends or family members be allowed to hunt? How often? How long? Also, some members may have the whole season to hunt; others will have only a weekend or two. Some will want to bowhunt only; others will opt for firearms. Who goes when? And where? Should there be a limit on the number of deer members of the group can take?

073 CHALLENGE THE BOSS BACHELOR

When you see half a dozen bucks hitting the same field day after day during the early season, it seems like tagging one of them should be a cakewalk. But bachelor groups are notorious for entering fields from unpredictable points—usually not close enough to your stand tree. You can steer those bucks right under your perch by making a mock scrape. Mature bucks are anxious to lay down the first scrapes of the year in order to show their authority over other members of the bachelor group. Your mock scrape will punch the dominance button of the boss buck by introducing a "stranger" who has the cojones to make a scrape on his turf. The dominant buck and his buddies will soon take it over and start hitting your scrape routinely when they visit that field. And if for some reason the mock scrape isn't enough of a challenge to pull those bucks close, stake a buck decoy right next to it.

074 GO LOCAL IF YOU CAN

If you already reside in good deer country, your best lease is often the one that's closest to home so that you won't waste all your precious hunting time on having to travel. Monitoring your own property—everything from food-plot maintenance to sweeping for trespassers—is much easier, too. Here are a few tactics for securing ground near home.

OBTAIN A PLAT BOOK This atlas of landowners and various property sizes (available from the county clerk or recorder) will help you to identify properties with the most potential by size and location.

MAKE PERSONAL VISITS Nothing beats a face-to-face meeting with the landowner. An introductory phone call can save time, though, and, in the case of absentee owners, may be your only option.

ADVERTISE A classified ad in the local paper can make some of those property owners come searching for you instead. Posters placed in stores, restaurants, and post offices can have the same effect. State that you are an ethical, respectful hunter seeking access and are willing to pay.

NETWORK Biologists, foresters, and employees of ag-related businesses or agencies can become great resources for any hunter. They're familiar with a wide range of local properties *and* their owners.

USE A SERVICE A good number of websites list properties available for lease by species, hunting implement, state, and cost. Some of these website services will charge a fee, but you get results quickly. It's certainly worth a little time on Google.

075 HUNT IN THE HEAT

Every early-season hunter who has walked away from a deer stand sweaty and empty-handed knows that high fall temperatures are all too likely to make whitetails become slugs. Nonetheless, you can score in beach weather, if you follow these hints.

SHADE If you hunt hilly or mountainous terrain, focus your efforts on shaded north slopes; on the other hand, if your hunting grounds are chalkboard-flat, concentrate on areas where a dense canopy of mature trees provides plenty of shade.

WATER Areas like wooded creeks and spring corridors are significantly cooler than surrounding uplands. What's more, they provide whitetails with the extra bit of drinking water they typically need in hot weather. The same is also true of lake, pond, and swamp edges, which will often feature dense, well-shaded bedding cover nearby, as well as convenient foods.

TIMING Dawn and dusk are the best times of day, of course, but pay special attention to subtle changes in the weather.

A breezy day, a slight drop in temperature, or an overcast sky can be a big difference. And if the forecast calls for a light rain or drizzle, then grab your rain suit and hit the woods. Nothing will get sluggish bucks moving like light precipitation—even if the mercury remains high.

APPROACH Hot-weather whitetails will move less frequently and cover less ground when they do move. This makes setting up tight to a buck's bedding area (without invading it) almost mandatory—which in turn will make an unobtrusive approach critical. If you're out hunting near a water source—as you should be—use a stream course as your entry and exit trail, or try to paddle a canoe across a lake or pond rather than just bungling in to your stand from the uplands. When hunting in north-slope timber, use the area's ridges to conceal your approach. Once you've found a promising location, don't give up on it just because your buck doesn't show up on the first day. The following day's forecast, even if it is only slightly different, could be different enough to put that deer in your sights.

076 SEE A GOOD MOON RISING

Early-season bucks routinely go between bed and feed, making this a great time to pattern your trophy. The big question is, when will the buck you're after be on his feet during daylight? According to Knight & Hale pro Chris Parrish, the answer is when the moon rises in late afternoon. So convinced is Parrish of this that he limits his early-season bowhunting to a single five-day stretch when the moon is right.

"Lunar activity is 100 percent critical after deer shed their velvet," says Parrish, who tagged 140- and 170-class bucks in the past two years on afternoon moonrises. "There's no better indicator of when big bucks will be on their feet and out feeding before dark." So, the $64,000 question is: How do you learn to hunt like Parrish? Here are the crucial steps.

STEP 1 In September, when it gets dark between 7:30 to 8 P.M., wait until you see the moon in the sky from 3 P.M. onward. An early moonrise now will have deer—especially mature bucks—hitting feeding fields way before dark. A good moon table can help you pinpoint the exact moonrise times for your part of the country. In states where hunting season opens later in fall, the next afternoon moonrise often takes place before the middle of October—still early enough for this approach.

STEP 2 Since you'll be locked into this rather unforgiving schedule, be prepared to hunt no matter what. Prepare backup plans in case of shifting winds, increasing temperatures, or changing food sources. If a hot spell hits, Parrish hunts near water sources he's identified ahead of time or on travel routes between water and food. He also scouts out fruit and mast production, which can change deer patterns. "Set up enough stands to let you account for every possibility, because just waiting until next week to hunt the right moon is not really an option," he says.

Also, because you're counting on the deer to feed earlier than they normally do, you can hunt closer to the grub than you otherwise might.

STEP 3 Stay dedicated to your mission. Parrish believes so strongly in this sort of approach that he avoids the temptation to stretch out his hunt if he fails to put a buck on the ground. "Hunt intelligently those five days and then back off until later if it doesn't pan out," he advises. "There's no reason to hunt deer that early if all you're going to do is educate them." Instead, you should catch them flat-footed when the next rising-moon cycle comes.

077 FOLLOW THE FAKE-DEER RULES

Most deer will show at least a little bit of curiosity about any decoy they see. But whether a buck will close in to bow range and give you a good shot usually comes down to your setup. Here are five rules—and their exceptions—for staking a fake.

USE A SUBDOMINANT BUCK Using doe decoys tends to attract does, which might hang around long enough to bust you. A subdominant buck decoy, on the other hand, tends to attract larger bucks looking to assert their dominance.

Two exceptions to this: When you're specifically targeting a giant buck, you may need to bust out a dominant deke. Also, it can pay to play the jealousy card during the rut by using a doe decoy or adding one to your buck setup.

FIND AN OPENING Keep your decoy in relatively open cover so bucks can spot it easily. Decoys placed in brush, tall grass, or dense timber can surprise—and thus spook—an approaching buck.

PUT IT 15 YARDS UPWIND Most interested bucks will approach the fake and circle tightly to get a few yards

downwind, putting them only about 10 yards from your stand—an easy chip shot. A few bucks will walk right up and face your fake. This setup puts them in easy range, too.

FACE IT QUARTERING TO YOU Even circling bucks will eventually approach your deke face to face. With your decoy quartering to you, he'll likely offer a perfect quartering-away shot.

One exception: When you're using a doe decoy, face it quartering away from your stand—because deer will likely approach this fake in just the opposite way, from the backside.

ELIMINATE ODOR You've seen what dogs do when they meet a new pup on the block. Deer are the same. Your decoy is going to get a thorough sniffing. So it's critical to eliminate (or at least mitigate) odors on the fake, whether it is human scent from carrying it in or exhaust from it being in the bed of your truck. My last step before I get into my stand is to spray my decoy down head-to-tail with scent-eliminating spray.

078 BLOW A BLEAT

I bleat a lot. In my opinion, this vocalization has the greatest upside as well as the smallest downside. In comparison to a grunt, growl, or snort-wheeze, and unlike antler rattling, bleats won't send a shy buck packing or run off a doe I might want to put in the freezer. And so, I always carry a can-style bleat call, which is easy to use and doesn't take up much space.

The only downside to a using a can call is that it's not very loud. So here's a trick. When you need a little extra volume—such as when your buck is off in the distance or shuffling through noisy leaves—instead of covering the hole with a fingertip, as usual, blow into the call. This not only allows for more volume; it lets you put some emotion into the call. Now you can make a loud, urgent-sounding bleat when you really need to get a buck's attention.

079

KNOW WHEN NOT TO USE A DECOY

There are some situations in which you really don't want to use that decoy. These include the following.

NO SURPRISES When you're not able to put the fake in a highly visible area, don't use it; bucks don't like to be surprised by decoys.

SHY BOY If you know you are dealing with a shy, nonconfrontational buck, leave the deke at home.

FEW TARGETS When your area has few bucks, don't risk running one of them off by intimidating it with a buck decoy.

080

BE READY FOR THE WIDE-CIRCLING BUCK

Early in the season, a buck is likely to waltz right up to a buck decoy or circle tightly. The pressured bucks that I've hunted, on the other hand, invariably circle downwind cautiously on a wide arc—at least 10 to 15 yards. In this case, if you stake your decoy 12 to 15 yards out, like most archers, that buck will end up behind you or at the trunk of your tree, making for difficult shooting.

If you're comfortable shooting to 30 yards or more, stake your fake between 20 and 25 yards from your stand. An aggressive buck that walks right up to the decoy is still in easy killing range, and a wide circling buck will cross right in front of your stand at about 10 yards.

081 TOTE A RACK

Real antlers pack more volume and produce a better sound than rattle bags, but toting a couple of main beams is inconvenient and noisy. Solve these problems by making a simple strap that lets you carry the antlers quietly and comfortably around your waist. Here's how.

STEP 1 Start with a rack that has at least three fighting tines on each side and is cut off (or shed) at the base. Brace one antler in a vise. Then, using a ¼-inch bit, drill a hole about 1 ½ inch deep into the bottom of the main beam.

STEP 2 With the antler still in the vise, screw a ¼x2-inch eye screw (available at hardware stores) into the hole, and use a sturdy pair of pliers to bend the eye of the screw open slightly to create a gap. Repeat steps 1 and 2 with the other antler.

STEP 3 Lay both antlers down on a bench or table. Slide the elastic section of a 24-inch bungee cord into the gap you made in the eye of each screw. Bend the eye closed again with the pliers.

STEP 4 Your antlers are now ready for the field. During bow season, tie them around your waist by stretching the bungee cord around your midsection like a belt, or use the bungee cord to lash the antlers to the outside of a day or fanny pack. (Make sure they're hidden during gun season.) When you get in your stand, tie the cord around the tree trunk to store the antlers, or use the hooks at each end of the cord to hang your horns on a nearby branch, where they'll be right at your fingertips.

082 GET REAL (OR NOT)

You've heard the standard tips for realistic rattling: Rake the antlers against a tree, then clash the horns for three 60-second bursts every 20 minutes, and finish with a series of deep grunts. Well, forget it!

Okay, don't totally forget it. There are definitely some times when this variety of ultrarealism is not over-the-top—namely, when you know a buck can hear you. In those cases, by all means, be the deer.

In other cases, the gospel according to outdoor writers doesn't warrant a literal reading on this topic. First of all, the basic premise is flawed. Raking branches, for example, is not necessarily more realistic. For those who insist it is, I invite them to explain this to those countless bucks that have skipped that step in a fight. Point is, buck battles are extremely variable.

Second, bucks do not read any outdoor magazines. They don't hang back listening for some deviation from the accepted rules of rattling before deciding whether or not they should commit. They hear you and they are interested, or they hear you and they're not interested, or just don't hear you at all.

In a great many situations—especially during the rut, when buck movement is unpredictable—you do not know that a buck can hear you. Rather, you are trying to get one to hear you as he passes through the area. So it makes no sense to conform to any particular rules of timing. Instead, keep it simple: Start out quietly in case there's a buck close and then rattle loud and rattle often.

When you're not smashing horns, focus on watching and listening for responding bucks—not fiddling with grunt calls and bleat cans and tree-raking. You can't be sure a buck has heard your rattling at this point, so why would you expect one to hear much quieter calls? Instead, save the subtlety for when you can actually see that a buck has responded, is close enough to hear softer calls, and needs extra coaxing to come into shooting range.

Until that happens, just keep banging those horns together.

083 CREEP IN FOR THE KILL

You've heard this old saw: "The first time you sit a spot is the best time to kill a buck." Actually, I've had more success during the second or third sit. Why? Because many times a buck will leave just enough sign to let you know that he uses an area, but not enough to pinpoint the one key place to tag him. If you get too aggressive on your first setup and bust the buck, your odds of tagging him there nosedive. So creep in instead, using your first setup primarily as a scouting location. Here's how.

SCOUT THE AREA Look for buck sign in order to determine two or three potential stand sites.

HANG BACK Place your stand in the least intrusive of these sites. Generally, it will be the one that's farthest from the bedding area and gives the buck the least chance of seeing or winding you—all while providing you a safe exit route. Ideally it also offers the best visibility; you want to see that buck if he makes a move.

HUNT THE SPOT If the buck comes through and offers you a shot, great. If not, don't worry. Odds are you'll spot him within a couple of sits. When you do, watch closely so you can pinpoint the perfect ambush point on his route.

RELOCATE If you saw the buck on a morning hunt, wait until you are sure he's bedded, then move your stand. If you saw him in the evening, then come back the next day, hang up the new set just prior to your hunt, and just wait for him to show.

084 GET DOWN

Call it freestyle ground hunting—a retro tactic that now has a growing population of bowhunters rediscovering the excitement in a nearly lost craft: fooling whitetails using nothing more than stealth, skill, and camo. No stand; no ground blind; just you and the deer. Fred Bear would smile.

Here are four tips for getting up close, getting drawn, and making the shot on an eye-level whitetail.

SEEK COVER Be sure to remember this handy saying: Cover behind makes the best blind. In practical terms, this means that in order to ambush a buck from the ground, you should be set up so you have mostly unobstructed shooting in front and good cover to the rear to break up your silhouette. I killed an Iowa 8-pointer years ago by backing up against a blowdown. Two years ago, I arrowed a doe from in front of an upturned root ball.

BLEND IN Use 3-D leaf camo or a gillie suit if you plan on doing as much stalking as sitting. Otherwise, standard camouflage will do just fine.

SIT TIGHT Bring a portable stool or seat. It's more comfortable than sitting on the ground and makes it easier to pivot, draw, and shoot. If you're still-hunting or stalking, shoot from your knees, which makes it harder for deer to recognize your form.

LOOK CLOSELY When setting up for an ambush, mentally mark the spots—a wide trunk, some low brush—where a buck's vision is obstructed enough for you to draw your bow. You may need to draw early. Or, if a buck surprises you, let him walk by, and double-lung him as he's quartering away.

085 GO GILLIE

Illinois whitetail expert Marc Anthony has arrowed three net Booners at eye level. His ground game is simple. He puts on a gillie suit and sneaks within bow range of giant bucks. The most difficult part for the bowhunter, he says, is realizing you don't need to be 20 feet up in a tree. "Like most archers, I began as a stand hunter. But the bucks were always passing out of range. One day, after watching a huge buck feed out into a beanfield, I got out of my stand and crawled toward him. Then, suddenly, he turned around and fed back at me as I kneeled there. I drew and killed him at 30 yards. That was it. I knew I didn't need to be confined to a stand anymore."

He starts, like anyone else, by working good cover. "I like wooded areas off field corners and especially on hillsides. In my experience, bucks rarely walk at the top or bottom of a hill. I focus on faint sidehill trails, which have been a big key to my hunting success."

With a gillie suit and a slow approach, Anthony sneaks right up on the bucks. "It may take me a couple of hours to move 80 yards. But if I see a buck, I just move right toward him." Breezy days are the best, he says, when ambient noise and movement help cover his own. "If there's a little bit of wind, I can draw on a buck at 10 yards, and he'll never even raise his head to look toward me."

Anthony never sits. If he has to wait a while in a promising spot, he usually just stands next to a tree that's at least as wide as his torso. "This hides my silhouette, but not my draw. In most cases, I let the buck walk slightly past me before I pull the bow back. I never take a shot at a deer beyond 30 yards, and most of my shots are 20 or under."

086 TRY THE EASY OAK HUNT

Ironically, smack in the middle of one of the season's toughest times (October lull) is one of the season's easiest opportunities. You can miss it completely if you're not paying attention. But if you are, if you monitor the oaks closely and are quick to notice when the deer suddenly shift their feeding focus to acorns, acorns, acorns—then you are in for a simple, high-odds hunt.

When deer start hammering the oaks, they usually tend to favor a single tree or clump of trees above all others. It's not hard to see it. Leaves are turned over, pawed, and indented with heavy tracks. The area is littered with droppings and partially eaten acorns. And this is key: Bucks often open brand-spanking new rubs and/or scrapes nearby—and at a time when only larger bucks are making such sign. The plan is simple. Hang up a stand right over the best sign in the afternoon and wait.

087
HUNT RUT RUBS AND SCRAPES

You've heard many times that bucks abandon rubs and scrapes once the breeding season kicks into full swing. That's largely true. But there are some important exceptions that can help put a rutting buck in your sights now. They are as follows.

CORE-AREA SIGN Most of the rubs and scrapes that a buck made in and around his core area during the pre-rut are ignored now. But even at the peak of the rut, a buck will still make regular return visits to his core area— and he may freshen those rubs and scrapes, or make new ones.

DOE-AREA SIGN Rutting bucks do also open new rubs and scrapes just off of prime doe feeding and bedding areas. This sign may be active for only for a short time, but it can draw visits from multiple bucks when a member of a doe family group is nearing or in estrus. Remember to keep an eye out for steaming hot rubs and scrapes to tip you off that bucks are active in the area right now, and to help pinpoint that activity. This can be a great place to hang your stand or to still-hunt if the wind is right. As with core areas, use trail cameras or speed-scout at midday to check for freshened spoor. With bucks preoccupied with does and moving unpredictably, you can get away with more intrusions—and hunting that fresh sign as soon as you find it can really pay off.

088
HUNT THE HIGH WIND

"A stiff breeze is the kiss of death for hunting on most days," according to Tim Walmsley, an Illinois whitetail expert. "But during the rut, I make sure I'm in the woods on a blustery day. Big deer will be moving."

But why would a rocking wind get bucks rolling? "First," says Walmsley, "high winds typically usher in a cold front following hot weather, offering physical relief for deer. Second, pre-estrus does, tired of being harassed by bucks, figure that they can escape their suitors more easily when wind covers their movement and noise, so they're up and about. Bucks will start catching whiffs of doe scent all over and will run around trying to find the females. This builds upon itself in layers until you get a kind of chaos."

Meanwhile, gusty conditions make it harder for deer to hear and easier for any hunters to go undetected. What's more, windy-day bucks tend to take refuge in predictable places, making them simpler to find. "They head to a valley, bowl, creekbottom, a stand of dense timber, or the lee side of a hill," Walmsley says.

"When the wind is pushing hard in one direction, I head straight toward these spots," he adds. Walmsley has found that it's helpful for him to listen to a radio to learn when the wind will hit. "As soon as it does, I pile out of my stand and nearly run to get closer to protected bedding cover, expecting bucks will move. I settle in until the action stops or I stop a buck."

089 GET A JUMP ON THE CHASE

The chase phase is the most exciting stage of the rut and a time when bucks are highly vulnerable. But it's all too brief and will be over before you know it if you don't pay strict attention and get ready to react.

WATCH AND LISTEN Ideally you'll see bucks dogging does. But finding kicked-up leaves or pine duff that reveals multiple sets of running tracks is another reliable indicator. You can also hear chasing: Hooves scampering over dry leaves, sticks breaking, a buck grunting, even a doe snorting or bawling. In short, it sounds like a deer stampede.

HANG WHERE IT'S HOT You can expect that area where you've identified chasing activity is going to stay hot for several days. So go back there with a climber or featherweight hang-on and set up for an ambush. Where exactly should you sit? Favor thick doe bedding cover, any natural travel lanes, or pinch points within the general area.

JOIN THE FRAY Another good option is to get even more aggressive, especially if you're gun hunting. If you see or hear a chase happening nearby and it doesn't seem like the deer will come your way, you'll want to hurry over and get involved. Remember, bucks are going nuts and does are in a panic, so they often won't notice you. Try to cut in front of the deer to get a shot. Or, just wait.

090 KILL A MIDDAY GIANT

Many hunters have found that midday hunting can be good during the rut, but whitetail expert Pat Hailstones of Cincinnati, Ohio, is fanatical about it: "Hunting early and late in the day is practically a waste of time now," he says. "I see plenty of little bucks then, but not the big boys. When the rut kicks into high gear, I usually sleep late." Don't think Hailstones lacks motivation. His passion for big bucks has helped him tag more than a dozen Pope & Young whitetails, including a pair of Booners. Most of them have fallen between 10 A.M. and 2 P.M.

"In 30 years of hunting, I've seen the same thing in every state I've hunted, including Ohio, Illinois, Kentucky, Missouri, and Kansas," he says. "Trophy bucks don't run helter-skelter early and late in the day like younger bucks do. The does are moving then, which makes them harder for bucks to find," Hailstones explains. "The bigger, smarter bucks wait for does to lie down for the day; then they rise and circle downwind of bedding areas to scent-check for does that have come into estrus." Hailstones intercepts midday bucks by setting treestands along overgrown fencerows and other funnels that connect doe bedding areas. To prevent the bucks from getting wise to his setups, he doesn't go near these stands until the breeding season begins. "Even at the peak of the rut, there will be days when you don't see anything at midday," Hailstones says. "But when a buck does come by your stand, it's going to be a good one."

091 CALL THE CHASE

In that frantic period just before the peak rut, when does are running from prying noses in every direction, calling bucks away from their hard-to-get girlfriends may seem like a tall order. In fact, the chase phase is one of the best times to talk a trophy into shooting range.

Not quite ready to be bred, does bolt away when suitors get too close. Invariably, some bucks temporarily lose contact with the female. Suddenly alone, they use all their senses to relocate the doe, making your estrous bleats and contact grunts potentially deadly.

But what if you don't have a grunt tube or bleat call handy? In that case, simply scuff the leaves to imitate the footfalls of a nearby doe. Lone bucks will react to the sound of another male, too, thinking he may be with a doe. So another good trick is to rub a dry stick against a sapling to imitate the sound of a buck taking out his frustrations on a young tree. Or rake leaf litter to sound like a buck making a scrape.

I always toss the duff high into the air, as the sound of debris pelting the forest floor seems to bring these bucks running. Just remember, when a wild-eyed bruiser charges your position looking for love, you'll want to either shoot or run. So be ready to shoot.

092 LEARN 5 LOCKDOWN SECRETS

Steve Snow doesn't sugarcoat the challenge of hunting the peak-breeding period, also known by many as the lockdown. "It's godawful horrible for about a week every fall," says the Iowa expert. But Snow, a 41-year-old bowhunter with some 40 P&Y bucks to his credit, isn't giving up; some of his most memorable bucks have come in a week that stymies many hunters.

START OVER Your first job is simply finding the deer. They might be just about anywhere, Snow says. To find them, you need to scout almost as if it's the preseason again by doing a lot of glassing and sitting in observation stands.

LITTLE BUCK = BIG BUCK Snow isn't after young bucks, but he doesn't ignore them. "Any time a mature buck has an estrous doe pinned down, there will usually be several smaller bucks nearby," he says. "If you watch them carefully, one will eventually wander too close to the big guy, who will stand up to warn him off and then lie back down."

WALK RIGHT IN If the habitat isn't good for glassing, Snow recommends walking to find bucks. "Once you start jumping does or small bucks you can set up a stand nearby or begin still-hunting the area immediately with a decent chance of getting lucky."

GO CRAZY With whitetails using offbeat covers, Snow isn't afraid to experiment. "For several years, I noticed bucks hanging near a lone maple in a CRP field during lockdown. I finally decided to hang a stand there, and I felt completely foolish doing it. Now I call that spot 'The Magic Tree.' Give me an east wind during peak breeding, and I just know I'll see a monster there."

TAKE IT TO 'EM When you do find peak-breeding bucks, quietly setting up and hunting a stand in the area can lead to a shot. But in the right conditions, Snow may sneak into bow range instead. "If you keep the wind in your favor and move slowly, you can get right in on them."

093 TAKE THE WHEEL

"Most deer drives are designed to push deer into open cover," says northern Wisconsin expert Tom VanDoorn, who has taken 30 big-woods bucks age 2 ½ years or older, including a 160-class P&Y. "But pressured bucks don't want to expose themselves. Rather, their instinct is to circle and hide." To counter this, VanDoorn employs a tactic he calls the wagon-wheel drive. "It's a drive in name only," he says. "You're not trying to push whitetails anywhere in particular; you're just bumping them up and letting them do what comes naturally."

First, grab a treestand. (Don't worry; nobody sits for long.) Then grab a buddy and walk to a clear-cut, swamp, or grown-over beaver pond where a stand tree offers decent shooting. Hang the stand, have your buddy climb in, and then you walk straight away from him on a line toward the most likely bedding cover, such as a clump of brush, a dry hummock in a swamp, or tall grass along a stream. "When you bump a buck, he'll run straight away to avoid the danger at first," says VanDoorn. "But then he'll circle back, potentially giving your buddy a shot."

Once you reach the edge of the thick cover, you just need to double back, switch roles with your partner, and repeat the process. Viewed from above, the paths of the drivers would look like spokes on a wagon wheel.

094 TAKE DRIVING LESSONS

How can you improve your driving skills? Pay attention to the following 10 lessons.

KEEP YOUR MOUTH SHUT Barking like a dog, whooping, or banging pots usually hurts your chances because it gives your exact position away. It's better to have a big buck guessing where you are. Plus, when he does move, you want him walking past the posters—not hightailing it because he's scared out of his wits.

STOP Instead of yelling or barking, you should halt your progress when you come to a promising thicket. A skulking buck will think you've seen him, get nervous, and get moving.

USE THE WIND Everyone knows they should post blockers downwind and drivers upwind. But you can actually use a breeze to your advantage before you even start the push. Have drivers get in position and just hang out upwind for a while. Their scent may be all it takes to nudge deer slowly past the posters.

FIND FUNNELS Funnels are fundamental to stand hunting, but deer also follow them when fleeing drivers.

KEEP OUT One of the surest ways to increase your driving success is to put a few choice areas of security cover off limits from day one. Bucks pressured elsewhere will move into your sanctuaries—and be there when you're finally ready to push it.

DRIVE IN REVERSE When you have a draw or a finger of woods that juts out from the main cover, you can try driving into the wind. That is, slowly still-hunt toward the narrow end of the draw or finger as another hunter or two posts downwind, just inside the main cover, to catch bucks slipping out the back door.

FIND NATURAL BLOCKERS Take advantage of any natural features that look likely to block bucks from fleeing in a given direction, thus helping steer them toward your posters.

POST BLOCKERS EARLY Sensing distant noise or movement, heavily hunted deer sometimes realize a drive is being set up and sneak out before it even starts.

WATCH THE WEATHER When it's snowing sideways, raining down buckets, brutally cold, or unusually hot, bucks tend to hole up in thickets, making drives especially productive.

YELL AT A BUCK Finally, if a driven buck comes screaming past you going too fast for a good shot, try yelling, "Hey, buck!" You've got nothing to lose, and he may pause to look or at least slow down, offering a better shot.

095 FIND THE SUPERFIELD

Every winter, state wildlife agencies field phone calls from people concerned about overpopulation because they see 30, 40, 50, or more deer feeding in single field. What they are seeing, in fact, is a prime agricultural food source that draws hordes of hungry whitetails from miles around. A "superfield." At first glance, superfields look like easy pickings. But big herds pose big problems for hunters, says whitetail researcher Grant Woods. "Fifty deer bring 50 noses and 100 eyes to bust you with," he says. "But that doesn't mean you can't score."

FIND THEM Simply drive around and look for big groups of deer hitting prime crops such as corn or winter wheat. Also, call a regional biologist who fields calls from the public. Getting permission can be easy, because when hordes of deer are ravaging one of their fields, farmers can be very obliging.

SCOUT THEM When you locate a superfield, scout it from afar. "If the deer catch your scent," says Woods, "you'll have instantly turned that field into a nocturnal feeding site." Instead, glass the area from a distance to pinpoint where the deer are entering the food source. "Then wait for plunging temperatures or an approaching storm to move in for an ambush." If you play it right, you should have dozens of deer heading your way with light to spare.

096 HIDE IN THE CORN

The one place guaranteed to draw winter deer is a standing cornfield, says David Schotte of Kansas's Blue River Whitetails. One of his favorite tactics is to drive around at midday to find a uncut field, get permission, and sit right in the crop with a pop-up blind. "These fields sustain lots of deer damage," says Schotte, "and farmers will usually let you hunt if you're willing to take a doe before shooting your buck."

Schotte looks for a field that abuts a wooded south-facing slope where deer will bed. Then he pinpoints the heaviest trails entering on the north side and sets up right in the stalks near the hottest feeding sign. "If there's one place where you can get away with setting up a blind and hunting it immediately, it's standing corn."

Use stalks already flattened by deer to completely camouflage your hideout. Then just sit back and wait for a hungry buck to show up.

097 CROWD A BUCK

"If I can't kill a late-season buck at a food source, I'll get aggressive and move in closer to his bed," says Tom Ware of Bucks BeWare Outfitters in Illinois's Pike County. "But I want to know that buck's every move before I make mine."

And for that, he has a plan: First, scout the field edge for big tracks and mount trail cameras to confirm exactly where a good buck enters the feeding area. That done, follow the buck's trail into the timber, placing cameras in promising spots, such as a secondary food source, a pinch point, or a fresh rub or scrape. Start out cautiously, penetrating only halfway or less to the buck's suspected bedding area. If you don't get pictures in the first two or three days, there's still time to move closer.

Keep hunting the field edge, as before—you might get lucky. But check your cameras daily, starting with the one closest to the field. "It's a big help to have a unit or an accessory that lets you view photos in the field," says Ware. "This way, you don't move any closer to the bedding area than you absolutely have to." All you need is one picture of your buck when he's moving through a given spot during shooting light, morning or evening. "Once you get it, forget the other cameras. Just go get a stand, put it up, and hunt it at the first opportunity. If he came through there once during daylight, there's a great chance he'll do it again."

098 WAKE UP BUCKS

If the tactics above don't work, or if the bucks sleep so close to a food source that they can see it from their bed, try this radical tactic: Barge right into the bedroom and scatter deer like a flock of turkeys. Sounds crazy, but I know of some hard-core hunters who make it work. They purposely bust late-season deer out of dense bedding cover and then set up an ambush for their return. This tactic works because when deer find a thick bedding area that keeps them safe through the heart of the season, especially one that has food close by, they don't leave it for long. The key to success is to make as light a scatter as possible. Approach the bed like you're hunting, with the wind in your favor. If the deer don't smell you, especially if just one deer's escape spooks the others, there's a great chance a nice doe or even a trophy buck will walk right back in and help you end the season right.

100
GET A SNOWBOUND BUCK

When deep snow blankets the landscape, bucks seem to vanish. Ironically, there may be no easier time to find them if you know what to look for. Here's your three-step plan for success.

STEP 1 The secret is to locate green browse. Thickets dotted with honeysuckle, galax, smilax, and certain species of rhododendron, mountain laurel, and greenbrier provide whitetails with protective cover and food when nothing else is available. Bucks love them.

STEP 2 Once you've located a promising thicket, expect a buck to lay-up in the thickest, lowest-lying part of it. Now look downwind from there for green browse, as well as fresh droppings, tracks, and trails. Set up and sit until dark.

STEP 3 If your buck doesn't show up on that first or second evening, increase your chances by inching closer to the low-lying bedding cover, looking for several trails that converge and lead directly toward the buck's lair. You are dangerously close now, so don't try to hang a stand. Just sit in a spot where you have a good vantage point but are also well hidden. If you busted that buck, you'll have to find a new thicket tomorrow. If you didn't, you'll have to find a taxidermist.

099 SHOVEL UP A BUCK

Clearing snow doesn't have to be a thankless chore. The trick is to bag the driveway and focus on your hunting property. Seriously, clearing trails through deep snow can help deer reach vital, dwindling food sources—and it can put a late-season buck in your lap. Simply clear some walking trails. Start at a feeding source and try to get within 150 to 200 yards of a good bedding area. That's close enough that deer will quickly pick up the trail, yet far enough that you're not apt to spook them. I've used an ATV or small tractor with a blade, a snow blower, leaf blower, shovel—even my feet. Then just set up an ambush. With dense whitetail populations in many areas, winter kills can be severe after deep snows. If I can help 20 or 30 deer reach a vital food source in difficult conditions and possibly harvest one mature buck out of those, I don't feel bad about it. You shouldn't either.

101 MEET BUCKS FOR A COLD LUNCH

The late season is a prime time to catch a big buck on its feet during the middle of the day. Hungry, worn-out post-rut bucks are more apt than usual to conserve fuel during the coldest parts of the day and feed heavily during the warmest—and have learned that they encounter fewer hunters at midday. Finally, does tend to feed early too, including late-cycling yearlings and fawns sure to draw the attention of the biggest bucks. For good feeding activity at midday, you want three things.

COLD Wait for a significant and preferably sustained drop in the mercury.

SNOW A snowfall really helps the hunter. It seems to strike panic in the deer, and they feed with abandon—often right through the middle of the day.

FOOD A concentrated, high-carb food source is essential. In farm country, this means mostly corn or soybeans but also newly seeded alfalfa. In the big woods, hit clear-cuts, oak stands, and treetops from freshly logged areas.

If you can put these three things together, putting together your hunt plan will be about as simple as it gets. Pinpoint the best feeding sign. (If you have snow, this should be a piece of cake.) Then simply set up between the grub and the most likely bedding cover, such as a nearby south-facing wooded slope. Finally, get to your spot well before the noon whistle. If you wait for the dinner bell, you'll probably be too late. Then just settle in and wait for a buck to show up for your lunch date.

102 GO FIELD HOPPING

Normally, Dr. Keith Chaffin watches just one prime feeding area during an afternoon hunt. But when the season is winding down, this Texas whitetail fanatic often checks several in a matter of hours, an aggressive approach that has produced some big bucks for him, including a 228-inch nontypical giant.

"The key is to have two or three choice evening feed sites located fairly close together," he says. Wheat, oat, or rye fields, food plots, and recently harvested cornfields are your best bets. And don't forget open oak flats and recently-logged sites where treetops provide browse.

Follow grassy ditches, thick hedgerows, or brushy fence lines that allow you to sneak toward one feeding area unseen, glass it thoroughly, slip away, and ease up to the next. Once you spot a good buck, simply slip in close enough for the shot. After a long season of sitting in one spot, Chaffin says, it's a great way to have a more active hunt and up your odds of getting within gun range of a late-season bruiser.

103 WALK IN CIRCLES

Only when you have exhausted hope of finding the next drop of blood in the immediate vicinity of the last should you risk leaving the main blood trail. And even then, you should do so little by little. First, clearly mark the last blood, and starting there, slowly walk in a gradually expanding cloverleaf pattern, looking for any sign of your deer. What you really want to find is more blood, so you can pick up the trail. Short of that, look for hoofprints, scuff marks, broken branches—any hint of your deer's direction of travel.

104 GET A FRIEND

The worst-case scenario when trailing a hit deer comes when you've searched hard, long, and ultimately in vain for the next drop of blood and you find no other clear indications of where your deer went. While it's not a bad idea to have a buddy along from the beginning of the trailing process, it is especially helpful at this point to get a friend or two. Line up—close together in thick cover, farther apart in thin—and methodically comb the area, looking for the deer. Pay special attention to blowdowns or thickets where a hit deer is apt to lie down, as well as any low areas, as mortally wounded deer tend to run downhill and often seek water. If all else fails, there is one friend to consider: man's best. Where legal, specially trained blood-trailing dogs can save the day and your venison. Call your local wildlife agency for details.

105 STAY ON THE BLOOD

Your hit deer is almost certainly lying at the end of the blood trail. This would be obvious to anyone under normal conditions. But shooting a deer can cause your adrenal gland to squirt gobs of high-octane liquid goofiness—or epinephrine—into your frontal lobe. So instead of staying on the blood trail, way too many hunters go bumbling out ahead, muttering things like "I'll bet he went on this trail" and "He's probably going to water" and "Are those scuff marks in the leaves up there?"

Listen to me: If in the excitement and stress of trailing a hit deer you can only remember one thing, remember this: Stay on the blood.

Even when the blood trail seems like it has come to an end, stay on it. This is really important: When you're standing over that "last drop" and wondering where on earth the deer went, nine times out of ten the answer lies not somewhere out in front of you but somewhere near your feet. Look closer. Get on your hands and knees. The deer may have taken a hard turn or doubled back some. Comb the area, for a half hour if needed, to find that next drop. It may lead to another, which may lead to your deer.

106 GET YOUR BUCK OUT

You've probably heard that the real work of deer hunting doesn't begin until your buck is down. That's often true. But with good planning, getting your deer out can still be relatively painless. The first thing to do is carefully map out the easiest way back to your vehicle or camp. Keep in mind that this is rarely the straightest path. Use the terrain and available trails to your advantage. If you expect the drag to be difficult, remember: This is why you have hunting buddies. Any of these three tools can help, too.

DRAGS The simplest commercial drags are basically a 9-inch rubber-coated handle attached to a loop of braided nylon. Wrap the loop around the base of a buck's antlers, pass the handle through the open end, and pull. Deluxe models may use an adjustable shoulder harness of 2-inch webbing, leaving your hands free to carry a gun or bow.

SLEDS Less compact but far more helpful are sleds. The best are constructed of smooth, durable plastic that rolls up into a packable, lightweight scroll. When unrolled and loaded down with a deer, they make bare ground feel as slick as snow and snow as slick as ice.

CARTS Wheeled game carts are the heaviest and most expensive haulers, but on relatively level ground, they provide the easiest going, and most fold up into a comparatively small and lightweight package that you can carry on your back into a wilderness base camp. With any luck, you'll be wheeling it out.

107 SKIN YOUR DEER

I hang my deer head down from a gambrel for cooling and aging, which keeps the blood from draining into the best meat. And I skin it that way, too, using these steps.

STEP 1 Lower the carcass so the hams are roughly eye level and the head is touching the ground, which helps keep the critter from swinging as you work.

STEP 2 Starting at the groin, slip your knife's point under the skin, blade up, and cut a long slit up from the bottom of one ham past the knee. Repeat on the other side. (Don't worry about hair on the meat during the skinning process, you'll rinse it before moving on to trimming.)

STEP 3 Loosen the skin around each knee and cut all the way around each joint. Grab and peel the skin off the back legs and down to the tail.

STEP 4 Sever the tailbone and then keep peeling all the way down to the front shoulders, using your knife when necessary to help free the skin.

STEP 5 Cut the front legs off at the knee. (It's good to have some sharp lopping shears handy for this.)

STEP 6 Starting at the chest opening, slip your knife under the skin and cut a long slit along the inside of each front leg to the severed end. Peel the skin off the legs, then over the shoulders, then all the way down to the base of the neck, using your knife as necessary.

STEP 7 Slice through the meat of the neck with a knife and cut through the spine with a saw.

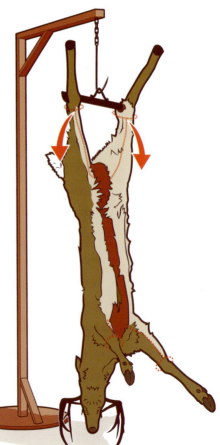

108 GET THE GOOD CUTS

Many processors offer bone-in cuts, but most do-it-yourselfers totally debone their meat instead. Here's what works for me. Start with two large, clean pans. One is for meat we'll categorize as "good"—the tougher, fattier, more sinewy portions that will become burger, sausage, jerky, stew meat, and pot roast. The second is for "best"—the larger, leaner, more tender cuts for steaks, dry roasts, and kabobs. Set that one aside for now.

STEP 1 Detach the front legs by pulling one away from the body while slicing between the leg and the rib cage. Continue cutting around the leg, eventually between the shoulder blade and the back. Repeat on the other side and set front legs aside.

STEP 2 Remove neck meat, brisket, and flank and toss into the pan. Since this will all be scrap meat, it's not important that you get it off in one nice piece. Hack it off the best you can.

STEP 3 Remove the shank meat on each hind leg. Now grab and remove all the meat from the front legs, putting it all, as well as any remaining edible meat on the carcass, into the good pan. Later, you can separate the best of it for stew meat and jerky.

109 BONE OUT THE BEST CUTS

After you've separated out the good-quality meat, it's time to grab that "best" pan. Start by removing the backstraps. For each, cut long slits from the rump to the base of the neck—one tight along the backbone, the other tight along the top of the ribs. Make a horizontal cut across these two slits at the base of the neck and lift the backstrap while scraping along the bone beneath with your knife to collect as much meat as possible.

On the rest of the hindquarter, natural seams of silverskin run between large muscles. Separate these muscles as much as possible by working wetted fingers into the seams. Then just cut the muscles off the bone to get largely seamless hunks of meat.

INDEX

A – B – C

Anthony, Marc, 85
antlers, 71
    See also rattling; shed
      hunting; velvet
beds and bedding behavior,
16, 20–22, 39, 41, 42, 43, 47,
96, 98
binoculars, 51, 52
blinds, 49
blood trails, 103–105
bowhunting, 48, 56–60,
63–65, 67, 70, 84–85
bucks
    bachelor groups of, 31, 73
    beds and bedding behavior
      of, 20–22, 47, 96–98
    core areas of, 32
    feeding behavior of, 101
    fighting behavior of, 31, 33
    hunt plans for, 16
    mature, 16, 30, 71, 73

personality traits in, 17, 31
ranges of, 30
response to calling, 78
response to decoys, 77–79
response to rattling, 81, 82
rubs and rubbing behavior,
    23, 24, 27, 87
rutting behavior of, 16, 25,
    26, 32, 33, 87, 89, 91, 90,
    92
scrapes and scraping
    behavior of, 25–27, 73, 87
social hierarchy among, 31,
    73
travel behavior of, 32, 89
bullets, 55
calling,14, 78
chasing phase of rut, 89, 91
cornfields, 96

D – E – F – G

D'Angelo, Gino, 10

decoys, 73, 77–79,
deer
    feeding behavior of, 18, 19,
      86
    sense of hearing in, 11
    sense of smell in, 9, 12, 13
    visual ability of, 10
    vocalizations of, 14
    See also bucks; does; fawns;
      whitetail deer
does
    and chasing phase of rut, 89,
      91
    in estrus, 87, 90
    visual ability of, 10
dogs
    following blood trails with,
      104
    sense of smell in, 9, 13
early-season hunting, 22, 73,
    75, 76
estrus, does in, 87, 90
feeding behavior, 18, 19, 37, 86,

CREDITS

FIELD&STREAM

Editor Anthony Licata
VP, Group Publisher Eric Zinczenko

2 Park Avenue
New York, NY 10016
www.fieldandstream.com

weldon**owen**

President, CEO Terry Newell
VP, Publisher Roger Shaw
Associate Publisher Mariah Bear
Project Editor Ian Cannon
Creative Director Kelly Booth
Art Director William Mack
Designer Barbara Genetin
Cover Design William Mack
Illustration Coordinator Conor Buckley
Production Director Chris Hemesath
Associate Production Director
Michelle Duggan

All of the material in this book was originally
published in *The Total Deer Hunter Manual*,
by Scott Bestul and Dave Hurteau.

Weldon Owen would like to thank
Bridget Fitzgerald for editorial assistance.

415 Jackson Street
San Francisco, CA 94111
www.weldonowen.com

BONNIER

Library of Congress Control Number
on file with the publisher.

ISBN 13: 978-1-61628-725-2
ISBN 10: 1-61628-725-x

10 9 8 7 6 5 4 3 2 1

2014 2015 2016 2017

Printed in China by 1010